INTERMITTENT FASTING FOR WOMEN OVER 50

The Ultimate Guide To Lose Weight

Author

Gertrude A. Ramos

TABLE OF CONTENTS

INTRODUCTION

Intermittent fasting is an eating practice that alternates between fasting and eating times. In other words, you should not eat at any time, but you should eat all your daily food at other times. This type of diet doesn't specify what food to eat, but when to eat it. The point here is to say that, in the true sense of the word, periodic fasting or Intermittent Fasting (IF) is not a diet, but a diet.

Periodic hunger is a practice in the course of human evolution. Supermarkets, refrigerators, or food were not available throughout the year for ancient people. They were not able to find anything to eat at times. As a result, people have evolved to function for long periods without food. Indeed, occasional fasting is more natural than ever eating 3-4 (or more) meals a day.

Anyone serious about lifting weights, exercise, and living a healthy lifestyle knows that the best way to build muscle mass and an aesthetically shaped body is to eat healthy foods and drink lots of protein.

But to build lean muscle mass is not enough. Nobody in the world can only lift muscles without fat. To remove the fat while making sure you don't lose muscle mass, you need to change your diet. This change is referred to as regular fasting. You should achieve this goal with this eating pattern. One study shows that periodic fasting or Intermittent Fasting (IF) causes less muscle loss than standard diets with limited calories.

Intermittent fasting (IF) is a dietary pattern that alternates between periods of hunger and a reduced diet, resulting in weight loss and better overall health.

The most common reason people use the diet form of "periodic fasting" is weight loss. This diet will cause you to eat less. This can lead to an involuntary decrease in the consumption of calories. This, in effect, results in a loss of weight. Of course, it all depends on you. For the rest of the time, you shouldn't overdo it.

For an extended period, when you have not eaten food, the body begins to look for other energy sources. The first thing he uses is in the form of glycogen and fat-stored carbohydrates. Regular fasting planned reduces glycogen and burns fatter. If you do your workout for the day at the end of your fasting, you're going to burn even more fat. For instance, if you haven't eaten anything since 6:00 p.m. the night before, you go to the gym at 8:00 a.m. fasting the following day and then your first meal at 10:00 a.m. So, you're doing 16 hours of daily fasting. This is the most popular method, as described above.

Periodic fasting or intermittent fasting (IF) will increase your metabolism marginally while allowing you to eat fewer calories. This is a very effective way of weight loss and fat burning.

Intermittent fasting may appear to be a good option for women who want to lose weight, but many wonder if women should fast. Is intermittent fasting beneficial to females? A few key studies on intermittent fasting have been published, and they can help shed some light on this fascinating new dietary trend.

Intermittent fasting has some advantages for women. The fact that women have a much higher fat proportion in their bodies makes it especially important for women trying to lose weight. When trying to lose weight, the body burns carbohydrate stores for the first 6 hours before switching to fat burning. Fasting is a viable option for women struggling with stubborn fat despite following a healthy diet and exercise plan.

CHAPTER ONE

WHAT IS THE INTERMITTENT FASTING?

As the name suggests, intermittent fasting consists of alternating periods of normal balanced eating, and short periods of fasting. The fasting periods are often between 12 and 16 hours, the "skipped" meal can be breakfast or dinner depending on your preference. Fasting enthusiasts mainly use it to lose weight, whether during a dry period for bodybuilding enthusiasts or when they simply want to lose weight.

Intermittent fasting includes alternating periods of feasting and famine in which you may eat as much as you like during the feast but only drink water during the fast. The goal is to achieve the calorie reduction benefits and use it as a tool to lose weight for some.

Intermittent fasting can be done over several days, alternating 24-hour cycles or hourly. The first option requires that you abstain from some or all meals one or more days of the week. Daily fasting involves 24 hours feeding and fasting cycles that start at the same time every day, e.g., fast from Monday 6 pm to Tuesday 6 pm, eat as much as you like from Tuesday 6 pm to Wednesday at 6 pm repeat the process. There is a short period of eating during the occasional intermittent fasting, usually 4-6 hours within the 24-hour day during which you can consume as much as you like.

Some of the things that put people off are the fear of being extremely hungry and not sticking to the plan or understanding how to fit it into your schedule. This is quite easy if you plan to eat your evening meal pretty much at the same time every day, but either side at an hour depending on whether you're doing an intermittent fasting or eating process. You can also handle socializing and dining out with a little preparation yet again.

Today, the most common IF protocols include fasting for 16 hours each day and restricting food intake to one or two days each week. If you consider intermittent fasting a normal part of the human eating pattern, then it can be said that humans are designed to implement it. Our hunter-gatherer ancestors probably did as well. Under this new plan, individuals who engage in planned intermittent fasting could potentially benefit their health in multiple ways, such as increased body composition, longer life span, and reduced aging.

While men may find intermittent fasting easier than women, there is some evidence that intermittent fasting may not be as beneficial for some women as it is for men.

When it comes to blood sugar control, it was found that women were negatively impacted after three weeks of intermittent fasting. However, men were not.

The internet is a wonderful place to look for information on almost any topic you might want to know about. Some women claim that after starting intermittent fasting, their menstrual cycles have changed.

Such changes occur because female bodies are extremely sensitive to caloric restriction.

When calorie intake is low, such as fasting for too long or frequently, the hypothalamus is affected.

The secretion of GnRH, a hormone that helps to release two reproductive hormones: LH and FSH can be interrupted (FSH).

Without a clear connection between the hypothalamus and the ovaries, it is difficult to determine whether you have regularly or irregularly timed periods, infertility, poor bone health, and other health problems.

Although human studies do not confirm the animal testing results, several additional types of scientific studies have validated the conclusions of these animal studies. While some researchers believe that fasting may result in a reduction in the size of the ovaries and disrupted reproductive cycles in rats, other researchers are skeptical of this claim and think that just a few weeks of alternating fasting reduces ovary size and irregular cycles in rats.

For these reasons, women should consider using a modified approach to intermittent fasting, such as having fewer days of fasting per period and shorter periods of fasting.

Fasting essentially allows the body to use stored energy, such as consuming excess body fat.

It is vital to understand that this is normal and that humans have adapted to move without having to suffer adverse health effects. All energy from the food is contained in body fat. If you don't feed, the body can actually' use' its fat for energy.

Life is about equilibrium. The strong and the bad.

By consuming more food energy is being absorbed than we can use. Some of that energy needs to be retained for later use. Insulin is the principal hormone involved in the production of food energy.

This helps to store excess sugar when consuming insulin in two different ways. Sugars in long chains can bind glycogen, which is then stored in the liver. Nevertheless, storage space is small and once it is full, the liver begins converting excess glucose into fat. This cycle is called de novo lipogenesis (which means "re-creating fat").

Some of the newly created fat is retained in the liver but most of it is transferred to other body fat stores. Though this process is more complicated, there is no limit to the amount of fat produced. There are two compatible feeding energy storage mechanisms in the body. One is very easy to access, but it has a limited storage capacity (glycogen) and the other is the hardest to reach. Still, it does have an unlimited storage capacity (body fat.)

The cycle works in reverse when we don't eat (fasting). Insulin levels drop, allowing the body to start burning stored energy since it no longer receives food. Glucose in the blood drops, and the body must pump glucose from the tank to use it as fat.

Glycogen is Energy's most open source. It breaks down into glucose molecules to provide energy to other cells. In this way, enough fuel can be supplied to the body for 24-36 hours. Instead, the body begins to break down to use fat as fuel.

So, the body can only be in two states: absorption (high insulin) and fasting (low insulin). Either we store the food energy, or we waste energy. It's one thing or another. If there is a balance between eating and fasting, then there is no net weight gain.

When we begin to eat from the moment we get up and don't stop until we go to sleep, we spend most of the time in the state of absorption. We'll gain weight over time. We left no time to burn food energy to the body.

To restore balance or lose weight, we simply need to increase the time we consume food energy. It is fast.

Fasting allows the body to use stored energy. After all, that is what it is about. You need to remember that nothing is wrong with this: that is how the body is designed. It's what dogs, cats, tigers, and bears do and we humans do.

When you eat regularly, as is often advised, the body uses the fuel from the food that comes in and does not consume the body fat, it will only store it. The body keeps it for when there is nothing to eat.

EFFECTS OF INTERMITTENT FASTING

Many studies have studied the effects of intermittent fasting on the human body in some of its modalities. More research is needed but the results are very promising: intermittent fasting causes blood insulin levels to drop, particularly after 16 hours of fasting, making it easier to burn fat and increase the growth hormone that builds muscles, strengthens the immune system, and regenerates joints. Short-term fasting induces autophagy in the brain, a mechanism by which neurons kill their harm.

Restricting the amount of food in worm and rat experiments, which can live twice as much, has been shown to prolong life. It seems that intermittent fasting works the same way but without a miserable life of constant hunger. Fasting activates sit-ins, proteins that control inflammation and aging, protects cells from oxidation and prevent cancer cells' proliferation.

Intermittent fasting tends to increase insulin sensitivity, reducing glucose levels, and thus could be used to avoid type 2 diabetes.

Intermittent fasting has been proven effective in reducing inflammation and oxidative stress, two of the trigger factors of cardiovascular disease.

Intermittent fasting decreases LDL cholesterol, raises cholesterol from HDL, reduces blood pressure and triglycerides to make matters worse.

Intermittent fasting succeeded in stopping Alzheimer's disease in rats and nine of the ten participants improved in a recent trial with human patients, thanks to the fasting program.

How to do it

It may not be easier to test the effects of intermittent fasting personally, but keep in mind these indications:

- Most of the fasting time at night is the most comfortable way. For example, the day you start, you usually eat at noon, and you no longer eat during the day. Skip breakfast the next day and eat at noon for the first time.

- Quick drinking water as if tomorrow wasn't there. You can also drink tea, coffee, and any liquid with no calories in general. No, it's impossible to add honey to the tea.

- Start with a day of weekly fasting. For instance, if you acclimatize well on Tuesday and Friday, you can do it on two non-consecutive days.

- Seek to be a day off on the day you start fasting from your workout program. The next day's trend, exercise just before the first meal.

- Avoid prolonged fasting exercise. Take a small portion of protein, a shake, or amino acid tablets that contain leucine if you exercise strength or intervals, so you stop burning muscle mass.

TYPE OF INTERMITTENT FASTING

METHOD 16/8

Achievements in art, athletics, acting, cooking, directing, and gardening are, for the most part, gained early in one's career. The process consists of 16hour fasting and the remaining 8-hour eating period during which you can eat normally.

This method suits most routines very well because of its practicality. But it only becomes an effective tool if you apply it the right way.

To be successful, mix the time you are sleeping with the time of your fast. Generally, at least that's what is recommended, your sleep should be 8 hours long.

So, it's been 8 hours of fasting without any effort. Now, if you are used to skipping your breakfast and eating only for lunch, it is very likely that you will easily adapt to the 16/8 method.

For example, suppose you have dinner at 8 pm and sleep there at midnight. So far, it's been four hours of fasting.

If you wake up at 8 am, skip your breakfast and have lunch at noon, you will finish at 4 pm fast without any problem.

People who don't like breakfast or who don't like it are the ones who benefit most from this method.

But even you who are not used to it can try. Sometimes it's just a matter of getting used to it.

It requires 24 hours of fasting once or twice a week. If you are a beginner, this type of fasting can be difficult.

You need to be very well prepared because a whole day without eating is a challenge that requires a lot of body resistance.

No solid food can be eaten during fasting. Everything that has a considerable caloric value - greater than 20 Kcal - should be avoided.

Drink only water, tea, or coffee without sugar, or sweeteners. After your 24hour fast, you can go back to eating as usual.

Before fasting, try to consume foods that contain plenty of protein and fiber so that you are fuller during the fast.

This is a great method for those who want to extend the benefits of autophagy - the process of cell renewal.

That's because it takes longer periods to occur and brings significant effects to your health.

Rejuvenation, increased longevity, cancer prevention, and treatment are some of the benefits of cell autophagy.

Anyway, if you are already adapted to intermittent fasting - withstand 24 hours of fasting - and want to enjoy the benefits of cell regeneration, 24hour fasting is a very interesting option.

The 5: 2 protocol is a modified version of the 24-hour fast. If it used to be about one to two whole days of fasting, here, on those days, it is allowed to consume a small number of calories.

The number of days you can fast remains the same. The only change is that you can now consume some calories on fasting days.

For women, around 500 Kcal per day is recommended. Men are recommended 600 Kcal daily.

Take great care with your food content and pay close attention to the way you distribute your calories throughout the day.

Give priority to foods that offer you a prolonged feeling of satiety.

In this way, instead of eating poor foods that may soon satisfy you, you are extending the duration of your fast and, consequently, receiving more benefits.

It is worth mentioning that if you divide your calories into small portions and consume them between short periods, for example, every 3 hours, the insulin spikes will diminish the full benefit of the benefits of fasting.

Try to have a maximum of two meals of 250 Kcal if you are a woman or two meals of 300 Kcal if you are a man. The time of these meals is up to you.

Beginners interested in fasting for 24 hours, even knowing their difficulty, should try this type at least once.

It is much more flexible and promotes significant weight loss.

As the name suggests, alternating fasting days boil down to taking turns between fasting days and regular feeding days. That is one day of fasting, one day of fasting, and so on, consecutively.

In the original model, you cannot consume anything other than liquids without calories. But other, more malleable versions break some of that constraint.

There are people who on fast days consume 25% (1/4) of their caloric needs. Others consume about 500 Kcal during fasting.

As previously stated, depending on how the calories are used, it is also much easier to practice alternating fasting days and enjoy their benefits.

Its main benefits are: great weight loss, decreased insulin resistance, more longevity, and heart health.

If you want to lose weight for an event that is close to happening, this method can help you stay in shape.

However, it is a model that, if followed as proposed by the standard version - 24 hours of fasting -, is extremely difficult to remain in the long term.

This depends on your body's adaptation to this type of eating pattern.

ONE DAILY MEAL

People, who love to test their limits, whether physical or mental, often eat a daily meal.

Currently, it is one of the most severe variations that exist. That's because you only have one hour to eat. The remaining 23 hours are done on an empty stomach.

The good thing is that there is a great incentive for you to eat healthy and complete foods since you only have one hour to meet your needs and prepare yourself again for another long journey.

Plus, you don't have to worry about what time you need to eat or how many meals you should eat.

So, those who have a very busy day today or for some reason are having a very busy day can take advantage of this method.

Eating a single meal every day is much easier since you are adept at the ketogenic diet.

The ketogenic diet changes your metabolism and, as it is based on higher consumption of healthy fats, you have more energy to perform your tasks.

Although a daily meal can provide some benefits, it is quite laborious to maintain such a model for a long time.

WARRIOR'S DIET

Developed by writer Ori Hofmekler, the warrior's diet consists of 20 hours of fasting and 4 hours of food.

It is possible to consume some foods derived from milk, such as cheese and

yogurt, vegetables, fruits, and boiled eggs during fasting. But they must be consumed in small quantities.

For the remaining 4 hours, you eat as much as you want. The author advises the consumption of natural and healthy products.

Although the foods suggested by Hofmekler have low concentrations of carbohydrates, if consumed in large amounts, they can break your fast.

The absence of limits makes the warrior's diet imprecise and arbitrary. Recommending eating a little something does not say what the exact amount is.

Even a fruit is capable of interrupting your fast, which slows down its speed of reaching ketosis. Remember that ketosis is the main cause of the benefits of intermittent fasting.

Therefore, some people are successful and others are not. Only those who calculate their macronutrients or those with luck in their favor receive benefits in this style.

But don't get discouraged. If you eat a diet, such as a ketogenic diet, which restricts and counts your carbohydrates, the warrior diet can help you lose weight, increase your energy and concentration.

For some people, it is very uncomfortable to go for long periods without eating. Now, imagine if they could not drink water or any other liquid during fasting.

Wouldn't it be sad? Yeah, well! This is how absolute fasting works. You simply choose the type of fast that meets your needs, the only restriction being not drinking water while you are fasting.

This certainly makes absolute fasting one of the most - if not the most radical types of intermittent fasting.

His followers believe that water scarcity accelerates three times the speed to achieve some benefits of fasting.

This is the case with weight loss in which, due to the lack of water, hydrogen atoms are removed from the fat to form H_2O molecules. As a result, you would burn more fat.

But so far there is no scientific evidence to prove whether this process occurs and, if it does, at what speed.

Furthermore, running out of water can put your life in danger. This is because the volume of water produced through fat is not sufficient to maintain its vital functions.

So, before trying a type like this, visit your doctor or nutritionist and check that there are no other more viable alternatives.

There is no one-size-fits-all strategy when it comes to dieting. This refers also

to extended fasting.

In general, women should approach fasting more relaxedly than men.

This could include shorter fasting times, fewer days of fasting, and eating a limited number of calories on fasting days.

Here are some of the best forms of female intermittent fasting:

- Crescendo method: fast from 12 to 16 hours for two or three days a week. Fasting days should be non-consecutive and evenly distributed throughout the week (e.g., Monday, Wednesday, and Friday).

- Eat (also called 24-hour protocol): a total fast of 24 hours once or twice a week (maximum twice a week for women). Start with fasts for 14 to 16 hours and gradually increase.

- Diet 5: 2 (also called "Quick Diet"): limit calories to 25% of the usual consumption (about 500 calories) for two days a week and eat "normally" for the other five days. Allow one day between fasting days.

- Modified fasting on alternate days: fasting on alternate days, but eating "normally" on days without fasting. It is allowed to consume 20 to 25% of the normal calorie intake (about 500 calories) on a fasting day.

- The 16/8 method (also called the "Lean gains method"): fast for 16 hours a day and eat all calories in an eight-hour window. Women are advised to start with a 14-hour fast and finally up to 16 hours.

Whatever your choice, during non-fasting periods, it is still essential to eat well. During non-fasting periods, if you consume many unhealthy, highcalorie foods, you may not experience the same weight loss and health benefits.

The best approach at the end of the day is the one you can tolerate and sustain in the long run, which does not have adverse health consequences.

For women, there are many ways of doing intermittent fasting. The 5: 2 diet, modified alternative day fasting, and the growth method are some of the best techniques

CHAPTER TWO

BENEFITS OF INTERMITTENT FASTING OVER 50

Heart disease is the number one cause of death in the world.

High blood pressure, high LDL cholesterol, and elevated triglyceride concentrations are some of the biggest risk factors for developing heart disease.

A research of 16 overweight men and women found an elevated rate that reduced blood pressure by 6 percent in just eight weeks.

Intermittent fasting in the same study decreased LDL cholesterol by 25% and triglycerides by 32%.

Nevertheless, the association between intermittent fasting and increased LDL cholesterol levels and triglycerides is not reliably clear.

Higher-quality studies with stronger methods are needed before researchers can fully understand the effects on intermittent fasting's heart health.

Intermittent fasting can also help manage and effectively reduce the risk of diabetes.

Some of the risk factors for diabetes appear to be reduced by intermittent fasting compared with extended caloric restriction.

This is done primarily by raising insulin levels and increasing insulin resistance.

In a randomized controlled study of more than 100 overweight or obese women, six months of intermittent fasting resulted in a 29% reduction in fasting insulin levels and a 19% reduction in insulin resistance. There was no change in the blood sugar levels.

Besides, it has been shown those 8 to 12 weeks of intermittent fasting in people with prediabetes decreases insulin levels by 20 to 31 percent and blood sugar levels by 3 to 6 percent, a disorder in which blood sugar levels are normal but not elevated. Just enough to diagnose diabetes. Nevertheless, intermittent fasting may not be as beneficial for women in terms of blood sugar as it is for men.

A small study showed that blood sugar regulation decreased for women after 22 days of fasting in alternating days, while men had no adverse effect on blood sugar. Because of this side effect, decreasing insulin and insulin resistance will probably reduce the risk of diabetes, especially in patients with pre-diabetes.

Intermittent fasting can be an easy and effective way to lose weight if done correctly, as regular short-term fasting can help you consume fewer calories and lose pounds.

Several studies suggest that intermittent fasting is as effective for short-term weight loss as conventional calorie-restricted diets.

A study of overweight adult research in 2018 showed that intermittent fasting resulted in an average weight loss of 6.8 kg over a 3 to 12-month period.

Another study found that intermittent fasting over 3 to 24 weeks in overweight or obese adults decreased body weight by 3 to 8 percent. The study also showed that participants decreased their waist diameter by 3–7 percent during the same period.

The study also showed that participants decreased their waist diameter by 3–7 percent during the same period.

It should be recalled that the long-term effects of intermittent fasting on weight loss for women have not yet been shown.

In the short term, intermittent fasting appears to help you lose weight. However, how much you lose depends on how many calories you eat during times without fasting, and how long you stick to the lifestyle.

Switching to intermittent fasting can help you eat less naturally.

One study found that when their food intake was restricted to a four-hour window, young men consumed 650 fewer calories per day.

Several studies in humans and animals suggest that intermittent fasting may also produce other health benefits.

Reduction of inflammation: some studies show that intermittent fasting can reduce the main inflammation markers. Chronic inflammation can lead to weight gain and some health issues.

Psychological well-being improvement: one study found eight weeks of intermittent fasting reduced depression and compulsive eating behaviors while improving obese adults ' body image.

Longer life: it was shown that intermittent fasting extended the shelf life of rats and mice by 33–83 percent. Humans have not yet determined the impacts on lifespan.

Preserve muscle mass: intermittent fasting tends to be more effective than constant calorie restriction in maintaining muscle mass. A higher muscle mass, even at rest, makes you burn more calories.

- This reduces insulin levels. This is rational because high levels of insulin hinder the release of accumulated body fat. When insulin levels are not quickly lowered, the body will not obtain energy from accumulated body fat.

- According to this study, the sensitivity of insulin increases when a person fasts intermittently. If the insulin sensitivity is low, the insulin cells in your body are not responding well. Insulin resistance is a factor that contributes to type 2 diabetes and also promotes fat storage. It increases your body's growth hormone.

- The amount of growth hormone induces the release of body fat and encourages muscle growth.

- You'll lose weight with normal calorie limits and intermittent fasting. Intermittent fasting though may increase the likelihood of muscle preservation by shredding body fat. This research and the personal results of Martin Berkhan indicate that intermittent fasting preserves a higher proportion of lean mass, rather than a daily caloric deficit.

- Cognitive effects: the increase in catecholamine fasting may positively affect the concentration and focus of the mind. You can also work for a long time, without worrying about food intake. These two things can combine to boost your productivity.

- Risk decreased for heart disease. Coronary heart disease is one of the leading causes of death among men and women worldwide.

- Promoting neuronic autophagy. Neuronal autophagy is the process of cells recycling waste materials and rebuilding themselves. Your brain's functions depend largely on neuronal highways. Eliminate this cycle and your brain won't do well.

- Increasing rapid BDNF levels (Brain-derived neurotropic factor). It fosters the formation of new neurons and synapses. Alzheimer's disease is associated with low BDNF rates and the rise of BDNF has neurological benefits to combat Alzheimer's disease.

- Ketosis: There may be sporadic ketosis. This is a system in which the body absorbs energy from stocks of fat. This sets off the keto.

- Increased ability to concentrate: from an evolutionary point of view, it is possible to think that after eating, certain cognitive functions are impaired. This is to be expected since after eating, the sympathetic nervous system necessary to start cognitive functions is deactivated and the parasympathetic is activated. Also, studies indicate that during fasting the levels of neurotransmitters associated with the psychological state of concentration increase, such as norepinephrine and orexin.

- It can enhance neuroplasticity, the brain's ability to create new connections. Entering ketosis and alternating between the different ways of obtaining energy stimulates brain plasticity.

- Protects against depression. There is a substance produced by the brain, BDNF (brain-derived neurotrophic factor) that is almost absent in depressed people. Boosting its production protects from depression. This can be enhanced by intermittent fasting.

- Protects against inflammatory processes. Inflammatory processes can interfere with the functioning of the nervous system. Faced with an inflammatory process, the body allocates its resources to fight inflammation and subtract cognitive functions. So, if we reduce the inflammation of the body, performing periods of fasting, we encourage those resources to be allocated to what is necessary.

- It can reduce the obsession with food and help us recognize hunger and satiety signals, helping to avoid emotional or boredom hunger.

- Reduces mental fatigue. The way we eat, especially if ultra-processed foods are included in our diet, produces insulin spikes responsible for mental fatigue. If after fasting we eat natural or "good processed" foods, these peaks are reduced.

There is no perfect way of example that also applies to extend fasting. Of course, to be efficient with this system, you also need to consider certain drawbacks from the very outset. Unless you feel that you can survive without games, then you're mistaken. The fasting time is only half as adequate without strength training and supplementary endurance activities. There's nothing in here, even without a predominantly healthy diet. Occasionally junk food is permitted, but it may not be scandalous. So, with that principle, you don't get a free pass to celebrate.

While it has a positive effect on most aspects of life, there are some notable downsides to becoming spiritually empowered. Doing this primarily if you are used to eating several times a day will help you get used to going several hours without eating. To a much greater extent, especially in the early stages, the threat is exceptionally great for those who enjoy feeling the epigastrium's discomfort, also known as the hunger pain. Conversion might increase the likelihood of a relapse. Still, intermittent fasting is not appropriate for those who have already overcome an acute eating disorder because it may lead to a new eating disorder. People with diabetes, because of the abrupt and substantial decrease in blood sugar levels, are not advised to go on an extended fast.

As an original form of human nutrition, fasting at intervals is not far from our internal conditioning. Consequently, the potential for weight loss success is excellent. And that the method works has already demonstrated hundreds of thousands of people. If you want to get rid of annoying body fat effectively and mentally rely on this nutritional form, you should give a fasting interval opportunity.

Lack of consensus about what constitutes a healthy diet also creates patient uncertainty. Is there a low-fat diet they should be on? Down with carbohydrates? Under-calorie? Down with sugar? Low on the glycaemic index? A radically different fasting approach makes it easier to understand. Two sentences suffice to describe it. Nothing to sleep. Drink water, tea, bone broth, or coffee.

That's all, diets can fail because of ineffectiveness, but also because they're not properly followed up. Fasting's most obvious advantage is its simplicity, which is the main reason for its effectiveness. The easier the better when it comes to the dietetic laws.

ADVANTAGE TWO: IT'S FREE

Of course, in an ideal world, everyone would eat organic vegetables and organic beef that had grazed near them instead of white bread or highly processed food. The fact remains that, sometimes, these organic foods will cost up to 10 times that of industrial food.

The government subsidizes cereals, making them far more competitive than other foodstuffs. For this reason, a kilo of cherries can cost € 8 or € 9 while a baguette is worth about € 1 and even less a packet of pasta. Feeding a family of pasta and white bread over a tight budget is much simpler.

No matter how efficient a scheme is when its costs are prohibitive. The price makes it unaffordable for those who can afford it. This should not allow them to have type 2 diabetes and its limitations.

Fasting is gratis. In reality, it doesn't just cost zero, it saves you money as you don't have to buy food at all! No expensive goods. No overpriced food supplement. No meal substitute or medicine. It's gratis.

ADVANTAGE THREE: IT'S PRACTICAL

Eating uncooked raw foods on your own is good for your health. Most people, however, have neither the time nor the inclination to make food every day. Time is the center of work, education, family, children, extracurricular activities, and personal activities. Cooking takes time, shopping, preparing the meal, without forgetting the time to cook and the time to clean it all. It takes time for everything, and time is a scarce commodity that is usually sorely lacking.

Even if it is with the best intention in the world, advising everyone to cook isn't the best strategy if you really want to get results. Fasting, by contrast, is the exact opposite: more shopping, more preparation ingredients, cooking, and cleaning. It's a way of simplifying your life. Fasting itself is convenient. Nothing to do. Many schemes give directions. Fasting needs nothing. Keeping it easier is hard!

ADVANTAGE FOUR: YOU CAN ENJOY THE LITTLE PLEASURES OF LIFE

Many diets recommend making the ice cream or dessert a definite cross. That's certainly good advice to lose weight. But putting it into practice is not easy. It goes on to abstain for six months or a year, but what about your remaining days? And then, why do you want to? Think a little over it. What could be more fun than sharing the assembled piece at your best friend's wedding and toasting with a glass of champagne? Want to abandon those pleasures forever? Instead of a birthday cake, choose a birthday salad? Existence loses its flavor a little bit, isn't it? There's a long time to live.

Fasting after occasional sprains helps restore balance. That is the essence of the cycle of life. Abundance carries on from drought. Starvation causes overflowing. It was always this way. Since time immemorial, feasts have always been celebrated with birthdays, weddings, parties, and other special occasions.

Nevertheless, such feasts must be accompanied by fasts. You can afford deviations by not eating as soon as you compensate them. Fasting is above all about equilibrium.

ADVANTAGE FIVE: IT'S POWERFUL

Many people with type 2 diabetes are considered overweight and have marked insulin resistance. Sometimes even a strict ketogenic diet (very few carbohydrates, not too much protein, and lots of fat) is not sufficiently powerful to cope with the condition. Fasting is the easiest and most effective way of reducing insulin and improving insulin resistance in those situations.

Fasting is independent, to conquer the stages during weight loss and raising the need for insulin.

The number of fasts that can be performed is not limited, and this is the main therapeutic benefit. The longest reported fast has lasted 382 days, with no detrimental effect on the patient. If it often happens that the quick doesn't yield the expected results, it's enough to increase the frequency or length until the target is achieved. By the way, diets — low in fat, low in carbohydrates (low carb,) or paleo — work for some people but not others. If you don't get any diet results, you'll have little leeway to make it more effective. On the other hand, with fasting, you just need to lengthen the time! The faster you go, the more likely you will lose weight, but it will always happen.

ADVANTAGE SIX: IT'S FLEXIBLE

Many diets recommend starting to eat in the morning, and then splitting meals by consuming the rest of the day every two-and-a-half hours. For some people, that type of diet works well. Nevertheless, finding and preparing something to eat six, seven, or eight times a day is extremely difficult. However, it is possible to fly for 16 hours or 16 days at any time. There is no set deadline. One day a week, 5 days the next week, then 2 days the next, you can fast. Fasting adapts to your responsibilities and enables several durations to be combined without being locked into a system.

If you live in the United States, the Netherlands, the United Arab Emirates, the polar Arctic desert, or Saudi Arabia's sandy desert, you can strong everywhere. Fasting makes your life simpler once again because you just have nothing to do. Where other proposals add complexity, it brings simplicity. If you don't feel well at some point in the fast, simply stop fasting. The malaise is going to go away.

Fasting's compatibility with all diets is its big asset. It does not impose any particular practice but, on the contrary, it consists of doing nothing.

- You're not eating meat? This isn't stopping you from fasting.

- You're not eating wheat? This isn't stopping you from fasting.

- Do you have an allergy to the dried fruit? This isn't stopping you from fasting.

- Short-term? This isn't stopping you from fasting.

- Are you running short? This isn't stopping you from fasting.

- Are you always on the go? This isn't stopping you from fasting.

- You're not sure how to cook? This isn't stopping you from fasting.

- Are you eighty-five years old? This doesn't deter you from fasting.

- Has difficulty chewed? This isn't stopping you from fasting.

Not eating for 16 hours is the trend: Intermittent fasting is the new miracle weapon for healthy and sustainable weight loss. Besides, the intermittent avoidance of food should inhibit inflammation in the body and lower blood pressure. A temporary hype or a sensible form of nutrition? Here you get the facts.

The intermittent fasting principle is explained in a few words: You do not consume food for 16 hours - except for water, unsweetened teas, and even black coffee. Drinking a lot is even a must. You can eat normally for the remaining 8 hours. There are no restrictions. Whether you skip breakfast or (late) dinner is also up to you.

If you eat food, it is broken down into its components and released into the bloodstream. If your food contains carbohydrates, your blood sugar level will also rise. To regulate this, your body releases more insulin to transport the sugar molecules from the blood to the cells needed (e.g., brain, heart, muscles). As long as blood sugar and insulin levels are elevated, your cells prefer to use sugar for energy. The fat burning then runs to a minimum.

If you forego food, the opposite is the case: blood sugar and insulin remain stable, your body increasingly relies on existing fat deposits. This increases your fat metabolism and relieves the digestive system. Other advantages: Interval fasting can inhibit inflammation, lower blood pressure, and promote new brain cells. Incidentally, it is not a new "invention". In the past, when people still had to get their food by hunting and gathering, they were used to long meal breaks and the body "optimized" for them.

Incidentally, intermittent fasting can help you lose weight sustainably and without the yo-yo effect. The prerequisite: a negative energy balance. In other words, you have to use up more energy than you take in. So, eat a balanced and wholesome diet in your eating phases and incorporate regular exercise into your everyday life. You don't want to do without morning exercise, but your first meal of the day is only "allowed" at noon? That's not a problem. On the contrary - training on an empty stomach has advantages.

If you stick to your stress areas, your training will be particularly effective. But you must train in your fat metabolism area. If you are on the go too intensely, the energy from burning fat is not enough. Since carbohydrates are not available, your body relies on muscle protein. This not only has a long-term negative effect on your muscle mass but also reduces performance and weakens your immune system.

The Best Intermittent Fasting Schedule? There is not any. Arrange your (non-) meal times in the way that is most comfortable for you. You can also vary the 16/8 shape. This is the most common, but alternatives such as 18/6 or 20/4 are also possible. Another option: You alternate between a fasting day and a "normal feeding day". Or you bet on "5-to-2" and fast 2 days a week and eat as usual on the remaining 5. Since intermittent fasting is not a diet, but rather a type of eating schedule, you can implement it permanently.

It is crucial that you feel good and can easily integrate your diet into your everyday life. If intermittent fasting means compulsion and stress for you, it does not make sense and will also have the opposite effect in terms of weight, because "stress hormones" promote sugar consumption and inhibit your fat burning

Intermittent fasting is a type of change in diet and lifestyle that, instead of drastically reducing calorie intake or skipping certain food groups, limits the times of the day you're going to eat and quickly. In general, fasting will include bedtime and avoid eating until the end of the period. There are many schemes to implement an intermittent fasting diet, and you should pair it with exercise or calorie restriction to reduce inflammation of body tissue. That can also lead to weight loss or muscle development.

Speak to your health care provider and explain why you plan to follow a fasting diet. Tell me about this diet's benefits and disadvantages, and let me know about any disease you may have.

This diet will make a big impact on the day's metabolism. If you are pregnant or in poor health, do not run without consulting your doctor first.

Caution: People with type 1 diabetes who adopt an intermittent fasting diet can find it difficult to control and maintain healthy insulin levels because they never can eat food.

When following this diet, you will stop eating for prolonged periods; typically, you will fast from 16 to 20 hours every 24 hours, or up to 23 hours, and in the remaining hour or the last 4 to 8 hours of the day, you will consume only full meals again. Intermittent fasting is usually a way to lose weight, and it is also an efficient way to regulate and schedule your food intake. Design and keep to a daily schedule will be critical. For example, you might slowly follow the diet by consuming only 2 meals per day.

Timetable your last meal every day at the time of eating.

That allows you to eat around 2000 calories if you're a man or 1500 if you're a woman. Eat 20 to 30 calorie snacks, or less, from time to time, until the quick ends. You can eat carrot or celery pieces; an apple quarter; 3 cherries, grapes, or raisins; 2 small cookies; or 30 g (1 oz) of chicken, fish, or similar meat. Most periodic fasting schedules are essentially the same as changing in just a few hours. You can choose from many feasible methods: a meal period: you can fast for 23 hours a day and choose to prepare and eat a healthy meal for 1 hour a day (e.g., from 6:00 pm to 7:00 pm).

Two meal periods: eat two healthy meals a day; e.g., one at midday and one at 7:00 pm. Now fast for 17 hours after the second meal, sleep, and do not consume the "breakfast" until the fasting period ends.

Days of omission: not consuming anything on Mondays and Thursdays, and eating healthy meals for 5 days. So, you could eat the last meal of your feeding time at 8:00 p.m. on Sunday. This is known as the 5:2 diets, which consist of eating 5 days and fasting in the other 2 days.

MINIMIZE YOUR DAILY CALORIE INTAKE

When you normally eat between 2,000 and 3,000 calories a day, you can reduce the number a little during the short meals. Don't exceed 1000 or 2000 calories a day. To achieve this goal, prepare a diet that includes healthy carbohydrates, excluding white bread and noodles but some complex carbohydrates and fats.

You'll need to eat all the daily calories during 1 or 2 hours of restricted feeding.

You will find that you eat fewer calories easily because you won't have time to do it during the week.

When you follow an intermittent fasting diet, you won't have to skip any particular food class (such as carbohydrates or fats). You can eat the same food types once you start your diet as long as you follow a balanced and healthy diet and don't reach 2,000 calories per day. A diet can alter eating habits, not the food types that you consume.

A balanced diet will only include small amounts of processed foods rich in sodium and added sugars. Reflect on nutritious proteins (such as poultry and fish foods), fruits, vegetables, and moderate levels of regular carbohydrates.

If you're not used to fasting, your appetite, thirst, and body system may be influenced by this diet. You will follow it slowly if you extend the hours of fasting between meals or if you start avoiding food entirely on one day of the week. This will help your body to detoxify and decrease the painful symptoms (such as nausea, low blood pressure, exhaustion, or irritability) that you feel.

At the start of this diet, you can also eat light snacks during fasting times. A 100-calorie protein and a fat snack (such as nuts, cheese, etc.) won't affect how well you start and keep fasting. So, you could eat some very light snacks.

As part of this process, you will need to gradually modify your diet to reduce your consumption of processed foods such as processed meats, milk, or soda.

Avoid the temptation of eating junk food, sugar, and processed foods in your last meal before fasting. Eat fresh fruits and vegetables, and plenty of protein, to maintain high levels of energy. For starters, your last meal could be a cooked chicken breast, a piece of garlic bread, and a salad made with roman lettuce, tomato, onion slices, and vinaigrette.

At the beginning of this method, some people eat compulsively but this will allow them to devote more time to food processing and less time to the "process of adaptation to fasting" of the food withdrawal period.

Eat a full meal until you start quickly. When you fill up before fasting, eating only sugar-rich foods and carbohydrates, you'll quickly feel hungry again. If you have a meal in your schedule, eat plenty of protein and fat. You might find it hard to maintain a very low intake of carbohydrates and fat, as you will always feel unhappy and hungry during the fast.

FAST DURING THE HOURS YOU SLEEP

This will be useful if you do a long fast not to think about the stomach's sounds. Every night you should sleep for at least 8 hours, fast for at least a couple of hours while awake or sleeping. That way, you won't feel deprived of food when you wake up because you will consume a hearty meal soon.

Upon fasting, the first meal or main course you eat will be your fasting reward. Upon fasting, you'll feel hungry, so you should eat a full meal.

You're going to fast most hours of the day if you adopt an intermittent fasting diet, but that doesn't mean you can stop drinking water. Besides, it will be important that you stay hydrated during fasting to ensure your body's proper functioning. Drink calorie-free water, herbal teas, and other beverages.

This will also keep you from feeling hunger pain if you stay hydrated, as the liquids will fill the abdomen area.

Fasting is known to be healthy, especially therapeutic fasting, intermittent fasting, and long-term fasting. Various ailments are alleviated, some illnesses are cured.

But what influence does a fasting period have on the hormonal balance? What happens to our hormones while we are fasting? Will fasting lead to aging faster because some nutrients may be missing?

Usually, one does not want to admit that aging is a part of our lives, but it affects every individual, with some being caught up with the aging process a little earlier, others later. At least that's the thesis.

It has become known that the reduction in the production of certain hormones begins around the age of 40 and is a major cause of aging. Regular fasting can have significant positive effects and largely reduce the signs of aging.

But what are the hormones on which, for example, 16/8 interval fasting has such a beneficial influence? Can you make general use of this knowledge? Is it possible to have a way of life where the negative influences of aging can be stopped?

Hormones determine our rhythm of life, whether it is growth, puberty, aging, inner balance, and even our health. In all areas of our life, hormones are involved in essential processes in the organism.

The proportion of the hormone DHEA produced in the adrenal glands begins to decline at the age of 25. Pronounced dehydroepiandrosterone, or DHEA for short, slows down the metabolism, reduces fat, and lowers blood pressure.

The two opponents' serotonin and adrenaline, which keep each other in check, are mostly known. With the stress hormone cortisol, which wants to convert everything into energy and makes sense in demanding situations, the DHEA slows down the increased energy burn and ensures a balanced energy balance.

You can visualize it like yin and yang, an image that stands for balance. If the production of DHEA drops, cortisone will likely gain the upper hand, which negatively affects the aging process.

But the sex hormones estrogen, progestin, and testosterone also decrease from around the age of 40. They are part of the tissue-maintaining and rejuvenating hormones. Other important hormones are serotonin and melatonin, the production of which also declines with age.

A list of important hormones that are involved in the aging process - or rather, it's slowing down:

- Serotonin (happiness hormone)

- Melatonin (sleep hormone)

- Estrogen (female cycle)

- Progestin (for water retention, female hormone)

- Testosterone (male sex hormone)

- Growth hormone STH (for body fat and muscle regulation)

- DHEA (slows down the metabolism)

On the other hand, adrenaline, noradrenaline, cortisol, and insulin (stress hormones) are unfavorable.

It is known that fasting has a positive effect on diseases such as rheumatism, arthritis, or osteoarthritis. This is related to an increase in the hormone cortisone administered in an artificial form in these diseases to curb the inflammation in the joints.

It is a reaction of the organism to the switch to the ketone metabolism, which initially means stress for the body. However, this diminishes as the fast continues and the cortisol level drops.

As the level of cortisol falls, so does the production of rejuvenating hormones such as DHEA and the growth hormone STH. The latter is even responsible for the fact that instead of muscle mass, fat tissue is broken down, which is very important in getting older. Because even from a distance, based on a person's silhouette, you can tell whether it is a young or older person.

Older people usually gain weight and build up fat deposits on the stomach, while at the same time losing muscle mass. This can lead to serious postural disorders and at some point, prevent you from getting up from the chair by yourself.

The sleep/happiness hormones melatonin and serotonin also boost their production to an appropriate extent during fasting. Especially in spring, the well-known springtime tiredness is quickly overcome with an internal spring cleaning through a fasting cure.

The serotonin level rises and the hormone melatonin ensures a particularly good sleep at night, which is also the cornerstone of a slowed down aging process.

It is amazing how positively our body reacts to fasting in many different ways and how fasting hormones control us:

- Weight loss and the state of ketosis lower blood sugar levels and regulate insulin production.

- Lowering cholesterol and thus lowering the inflammatory parameters and strengthening the cardiovascular system.

- Strengthening the entire immune system with improved digestion and the associated defense against tumors and infections.

- Increase in rejuvenating hormones like DHEA or STH and decrease in the stress hormones adrenaline and cortisol.

- Increase in well-being and a good mood thanks to the happiness hormone serotonin.

- Improvement of sleep quality through a balanced melatonin balance, resulting in increased stress resilience in everyday life.

- Improvement and balance of the necessary sex hormones such as estrogens and testosterone also have a rejuvenating effect on men's and women's bodies and minds.

FASTING HORMONES - THE BOTTOM LINE

Regular fasting cures positively influence the body, regardless of your age or health situation.

Therapeutic fasting cures or intermittent fasting have a rejuvenating effect. But not only that, the hormonal balance is a very complex system, which can be unbalanced by stress or poor nutrition.

An annual fast is the best option here. Possible complaints and illnesses can certainly be associated with a disturbed hormonal balance, which can be brought back into balance by a regular fasting period.

It is not for nothing that many people see their younger, firmer skin, a special glow of the eyes, and shiny hair after the fast.

It is not a free ticket to eternal life. Still, fasting offers a completely natural opportunity to live happily and healthily with aging and at the same time with a balanced hormone balance. No matter what phase of life you are in.

CHAPTER FOUR

HOW THE BODY PRODUCES ENERGY WITH INTERMITTENT FASTING?

Intermittent fasting is a very important tool for weight loss and health. It is about staying the day without eating. There are several ways to be done, starting in 12 hours up to 24 hours, 36 hours of fasting. Each one chooses the period that best suits their day, the use of 16-hour intermittent fasting being very common. However, many people are concerned about how our body produces energy with intermittent fasting. Many would still like to know how many hours our bodies start burning fat as the main fuel and how to manage it.

BURNING GLUCOSE FROM FOOD

Up to four hours after a meal, your body gets the energy to perform its functions through the glucose obtained from food.

This glucose is obtained mainly from carbohydrates present in sweet, floury, industrialized foods, pasta, and potatoes.

The best thing for your health would be to get good carbohydrates from fruits and vegetables.

These foods are digested in our digestive system until they turn into glucose and are absorbed from the intestine into the blood.

When this exogenous glucose is used as an energy source, this period can be prolonged or shortened according to the control of your food regarding these types of foods.

Having a restricted carbohydrate diet, the body's period uses the glucose that comes from the diet as energy will be shorter.

If the glucose ingested at the last meal is too large, it is also stored as fat or glycogen and is not immediately used as an energy source.

BURNING GLUCOSE FROM GLYCOGEN

After the period in which the body has used all the available glucose from the food and you continue on Intermittent Fasting, it starts using glycogen as an energy source.

Glycogen is a polysaccharide, formed from excess glucose from food, which works as a form of energy store in our liver and muscles.

This sugar is broken down and releases glucose to our body to be used as energy for our functions.

In this breakdown of glycogen, water molecules are released and eliminated from our body.

This leads to a loss of weight from our bodies.

However, in this initial phase, it is only a loss of water and not fat.

Glycogen has a limited supply that tends to last up to 24 to 28 hours in maintaining our metabolism.

Physical activities, lean body composition, and other hormonal factors vary this period of glycogen duration.

BURNING GLUCOSE FROM GLYCOGEN AND FAT

The burning of fat as an energy source for the body does not start only after zeroing the glycogen supply.

It starts from four hours after the last feeding when the meal's glucose is depleted as fuel.

This burning of fat through gluconeogenesis, where fat is converted to glucose, remains increasing until the peak around two days.

In this period, it is observed that up to 16 hours of fasting the use of glycogen as an energy source is greater than fat.

After this period, the inversion occurs.

With that, fat becomes the main energy source for our body.

What is found is that most tissues continue to use glucose from glycogen.

However, muscles, liver, and fat cells are already beginning to use fat as an energy source.

LOSE WEIGHT THROUGH AN INTERMITTENT FASTING DIET

Intermittent weight loss from fasting is a technique that has become popular over the past few years. It's a method of eating where you switch from feeding to fasting. You get to schedule your times of fasting and nonfasting, in which you drink only water. Although it is unnecessary to do intermittent fasting every other day to lose weight, it is advised for those who want to lose weight, at least twice a week.

With an intermittent fasting diet, you are allowed to eat anything you wish in the periods when you are not fasting. You'll stick to healthy foods if you're looking to lose weight and avoid those that will defeat the whole process's purpose. During this time, it is recommended that you take carbohydrates as they help with fat metabolism. Drinking water is highly encouraged when you are fasting, as staying hydrated helps you lose weight more quickly. After all, you can go without food for days, but not without water.

Over the years, fasting has helped many people lose weight, and keep it off. There are a lot of reasons why it's one of the easiest ways to get into shape. If you cut your calories by continuing through scheduled fasting times, the body is forced to provide nutrition from its reserves, usually fat. Because weight loss means eating less than you're consuming, fasting lets you focus more on exercise than on a diet.

With intermittent fasting, you get relative freedom with what you eat. This is different from the many fad diets where you're limited to certain types of food. Although freedom is provided, you should only take what's right for you, as mentioned earlier. Include plenty of fiber in your diet, as it means that your body is fully working. You have to establish and stick to some sort of plan for intermittent fasting to lose weight to work. A present intermittent fasting diet plan is hard to follow, as it might not work into your lifestyle. Instead, set your days of fasting and non-fasting.

To get the hang of intermittent fasting and how weight loss happens in the everyday lifestyle with its definition, here is a summary of how to do it and take advantage of it.

It is possible to agree on several forms of intermittent fasting cycles, some differ from 24 hours plus eating on Tuesday at 6 pm and then taking the next meal on Wednesday at 6 pm. A quick that shouldn't be marketed as such for long as it impacts the metabolic rate and deteriorates health in turn. The best option is to choose a 12-hour period, where fasting takes place for half a day, and then any fat or carbohydrate food beneficial to the body.

What happens when one meal is taken is that the body uses it until the next 12 hours and the calorie stored as fat is consumed and used by the body when digested. It results in weight loss, and after a while, the desire and hunger pangs will also vanish as the body becomes used to it.

Weight loss through intermittent fasting occurs only when it is regularly practiced. There should be a plan for consistency that is simple and easily followed daily. Set food groups at intervals of 12 hours, and just have those. A simple balance of the groups will decide the intake of food necessary for the well-being of the body, healthy metabolism, and ultimately weight burning out unexpectedly. Calcium, sugar, carbohydrates, and fats can be found in the community. The only thing to do is manage it properly.

Intermittent fasting molds the body's needs in a way where regular snacking needs naturally die down. What happens is when extra meal intake and fat were stored in the body, that particular time is simply cut off from the daily routine and weight loss begins to occur with it. The stress that the body takes in the production, absorption and use of the food, and extra meal in the consumption is also decreased, instead, the same amount of energy is used to absorb the stored calories and burn it down by reducing fat on the stomach other body parts.

BLOOD SUGAR LEVELS AND ROUTINES ARE ADJUSTED APPROPRIATELY

There are several benefits of intermittent fasting and one of them is healthy blood sugar levels as the body's intake decreases. Studies show that fewer cravings occur and this type of diet also regulates blood pressure, stress, and heart disease apart from sugar level. Not only would intensive workouts be avoided and drastic diet cuts would not occur, but eating just about everything you want and still weight reduction happens in a span of a few months. Also, more healthy food intake and a nutrient developed over a period that is tough to make a habit of when IF is not followed.

Regardless of how busy you are, you must exercise every day if you want to lose weight and not recover from the weight loss. Your simple act of walking to the store instead of driving can greatly impact how quickly you lose weight.

- Housework exercise: As many as you can mount the stairs, walk the dog three times a day, shake, sweep, and mop vigorously.

- Increasing your stage number: Instead of elevator and park, use the stairs from the store as far as possible.

Start making a hobby involving moving a little while, though it doesn't seem proper exercise. Gardening, small projects, car work, or animal play are excellent ways to burn calories.

When you try to lose weight quickly for a particular event and don't mind losing lost weight you should want a streamlined exercise routine. Most women's and fitness websites, such as personal trainers, offer similar streamlined workout routines designed to maximize weight loss and make weight loss noticeable within a few days of starting the regimen.

If you are interested in losing weight and not regaining your weight, you will have to do more than a condensed exercise program. Starting with the activities you want to do and finding fun ways to do them is the best way to get started. Choosing an exercise, you enjoy does not necessitate much additional motivation every day, because you do not need that much motivation each day if you choose an exercise you enjoy. Instead, try out various exercises until you find one that you like, such as swimming, cycling, or even Zumba.

Remember that games like volleyball, tennis, and even Frisbee (frisbee) can help you burn calories while having fun to the fullest. Hence, exercise is a fun and social activity that you will want to enjoy every day.

The best form of fitness training is to include low and high-intensity aerobic exercises for the best results.

While combining cardiovascular training with resistance training is important for the body's overall health, cardiovascular training will help you lose weight quickly. Weight resistance training won't help you lose weight overnight but it can make your metabolism's energy use more effective.

Variety is the key to keeping you happy and enjoying a healthier life. You run a higher risk of injuring yourself if you do the same exercises every day. You are also more likely to get bored, so finding the motivation to continue the exercise will be more difficult. If you're in the gym, change machines, participate in a gym class and add to your routine some resistance training.

Perform aerobic activities of low impact. Moderate aerobic exercises involving brisk walking, cycling, aerobic machines, or swimming, burning calories, and keeping the heart healthy.

Resistance training and weight training are beneficial for people trying to lose weight because it builds muscles and increases metabolism. Approximately double calorie expenditure is achieved when aerobics and weight training are combined with weight loss strategies.

Rest between each strength training session of the same muscle group for at least 24 to 48 hours and take 1 or 2 days off every week. You thereby exercise all muscle groups and at the same time burn calories with more muscles, as if you were doing several things concurrently with the workout.

Adequate rest will help you maintain sufficient energy all day long, making you less likely to over-eat and hurt yourself during physical activity. Sleep deprivation was associated with the inability to lose fat, so getting enough sleep can support you on the road to weight loss.

Before choosing what kind of intermittent fasting to practice, you know the ERRORS that can ruin your health and stagnate in weight loss.

Women are very different from men when it comes to hormones and muscle mass, so we have to practice intermittent fasting differently. If you don't pay attention to these errors, you're going to fall into the same trap that many women are falling into. You're going to end up frustrated and wonder why it doesn't work for you or why you're feeling worse than you started.

So, let's move on to the mistakes women make when carrying out intermittent fasting.

DO NOT GRADUALLY STORE!!! If you're not used to making long and sudden fasts for 16-24 hours, your body's going to experience a shock and your hormones are going to leave equilibrium. This can hurt your metabolism and you will end up depressed and sick rather than losing weight.

Continue to introduce intermittent fasting slowly. Compress the time window you eat slowly and increasing the time window you are fasting in.

For example, if you're used to dinner at 8 p.m. and breakfast at 6 a.m. the next day, then try dinner at 6 p.m. this week and have breakfast at 6 a.m.
This will increase your fasting window from 10 hours to a 12-hour window. Do it for 1 week and evaluate how you feel!

If you don't experience many cravings, headaches, or any other negative symptoms, then increase your fasting hours by 1 or 2 more hours the following week.

DO NOT LIST YOUR SERVICE! This is one of the WORST errors that you can make. Most women choose to fast for 18 hours, and while their body screams that they are starving, they do not eat even if they feel weak because 18 hours have not gone by.

What a fatal error!

This is the only thing that causes slow metabolism and the body sticks to fat.

This is why you should always listen to your body. Follow the intermittent fasting method of intuition. Let you be driven by your body! Hear the signals your body is giving you ALL TIMES!

If when you are doing an X hour of fasting you feel weak, you have headaches, you are hungry excessively, you feel that you are going to pass out, or that you want to vomit... ALL these are symptoms that you are exceeding yourself in the number of hours of fast what are you doing and what do you need to eat?

This does not mean that you will never be able to fast for X hours. It just means that your body is not yet ready for such a long fast and that you have to start with a slightly shorter fast which you will gradually increase.

THE SAME AS MEN OR THE SAME AS WOMEN! As a woman, finding the type of fasting that fits our lifestyle and body type best is MUST IMPORTANT. Generally speaking, what works for men does not work for women. It may not work for you what works for me! We are all different, and the speed that suits your body best may vary from your mate, neighbor, aunt, etc. So, try different schedules to see which one is best for you and which one fits with your daily activities. Try versatility.

For example, if you usually have dinner at 6 p.m. and have breakfast at 10 a.m. the next day, but today you have an event with friends where you'll have dinner until 8 p.m. You can have dinner at 8 pm and switch your lunch for midday or just fast a little shorter the next day. NOTHING IF YOU MOVE THE SCHEDULE A LITTLE LESS!

You don't have to fast every day for 16, 18, 20, or 24 hours! You can vary the hours of fasting that you do every day.

The hours of fasting that I do daily vary depending on how hungry I am or what activities I have that day. This gives me the flexibility to feel good at all times in my body.

DO THE FAST OF THE KETOGENIC DIET! Do NOT fly with the ketogenic diet intermittently! It's going to be a huge shock to your skin. If you have been practicing the ketogenic diet for a while now, then you can begin to implement intermittent fasting. However, if you're a ketogenic diet beginner, let your body first adjust to this new eating style and then introduce intermittent fasting.

When you introduce these concurrently, the body will resist so many changes and try to protect itself by sticking to the food and nutrients it receives rather than using them freely.

Even I would recommend starting with the ketogenic diet first and then adding intermittent fasting after a few months of practicing the ketogenic diet.

With the ketogenic diet, you will receive far more health benefits and weight loss than with intermittent fasting. This does not mean intermittent fasting is not a fabulous tool for burning fat and health... It just means it's a more advanced tool to give our metabolism an extra boost once it's in a fatburning mode and on the way to better health

Studies on the potential benefits of fasting have emerged in recent years, particularly since the 2016 Nobel Prize was awarded to the Japanese Yoshinori Ohsumi medical team to discover the health benefits of the metabolic process called autophagy. It is a method by which the body is able to eliminate aberrant structures, so that altered or tumor cells, viruses, bacteria, and other structures are simply "engulfed" by lysosomes, macrophages, and other immune system-derived processes that occur mainly in periods of fasting. It has been observed that autophagy occurs in the body after approximately 12 hours of fasting due to the activation of the AMPK metabolic pathway when glucose and insulin are at low levels.

Without a doubt, both metabolic syndrome and all associated processes can be improved thanks to fasting. For example:

- Blood glucose and insulin fasting.

- HDL lipoprotein boost.

- Reduced visceral fat and lower triglycerides.

- Blood pressure control.

- Blood coagulation improvement and thrombosis and cardiovasculardisease prevention.

- Development of the predisposition of metabolic syndrome-associatedbenign and malignant tumors.

Some studies have an influence with respect to different cholesterol fractions on the positive effect of fasting so that LDL appears to decrease and HDL to increase.

INTERMITTENT FASTING AND BLOOD PRESSURE

Although there are no official trials in which increases in blood pressure have been shown in intermittent fasting, we find that patients who have been consumed or gradually decreasing calories for several days have more than apparent a drop in blood pressure. Up to 80% of subjects experience a significant drop in blood pressure from 3 or 4 days of fasting. We must bear in mind that when a person fasts insulin levels tend to decrease because we know that insulin is pro-inflammatory, it increases sodium retention and helps to produce fluid retention in the body, which also allows fasting and blood pressure to decrease.

It should be remembered that one of the benefits of trying to limit the number of calories to 8-10 hours is that people usually end up consuming less. The studies conducted by Varady Et. Al in 2013 found that for 12 weeks the correlation between a group of people who ate food for many hours and another who practiced intermittent fasting resulted in an average reduction of 5.2 kg between the second of the listed groups after a few weeks. A fat reduction of 3.6 kg has also been observed, which is explained by the fact that there are more hours of low insulin levels when fasting, which promotes metabolic activation associated with fat loss.

Some athletes are afraid that the fasting will result in a loss of muscle mass caused by proteolysis, however, numerous studies have been conducted in which the amount of nitrogen in urea (a good indicator of proteolysis) has been tested, concluding that it does not increase until 60 hours of fasting, so there should be no concern about the loss of muscle mass.

An interesting fact demonstrated by the scientist is that when undergoing an obese population nucleus, they both lose the same amount of weight relative to another group that performs fasting. Those who practiced intermittent fasting, however, decreased more kilos associated with fat mass (90%) compared with fat-free mass (10%). The group which performed a continuous caloric restriction lost 75% of weight in fat mass and up to 25% of fat-free mass, which means greater muscle mass loss and appears to achieve a lower basal metabolic rate after a few weeks (as opposed to those that perform intermittent fasting).

People who make an ongoing caloric restriction have more problems with increased appetite, heart output, thyroid-level hormonal imbalances, growth hormone, glucagon, adrenaline, testosterone, etc. This does not happen, and even some parameters improve in people accustomed to fasting. We also know that in subjects who perform fasting levels of leptin, ghrelin or adiponectin tend to be much more regulated, which means that appetite and satiety balance are more controlled because these hormones are directly responsible for these sensations.

We're stopping at people fasting in Ramadan. Modulation and enhancement of inflammation-related biomarkers (such as C-reactive protein, interline 6, or Alfa tumor necrosis factor) were observed. People who made Ramadan appeared to lower the body's levels of inflammation. We find that the activity of the AMPK enzyme pathway increases after 12 hours of fasting, consistent with autophagy and immune system regulation with reduced body inflammation.

Intermittent fasting imposes a diurnal pattern on the organism's food consumption, which makes the person better adapt to the biological cycles of day/night, the organism consumes food for 8 hours a day, and in effect states that the intake will not be done during the following 16 hours. The body recognizes eating during daylight hours and the hypothalamus receives an activation that has a very positive effect on the rest of the glandular, hormonal and immunological function.

The digestive system is one of the systems that most benefit from regulating circadian rhythms, as many of its functions are closely related to these rhythms. For example, stomach emptying, blood flow at mesenteric vessel level (which must be higher during the day than at night), as well as all metabolic functions associated with the pancreas, gallbladder, or liver. This allows all digestive metabolic functions to be active during the day and slow them down at night.

Likewise, it has been shown that when at night food is ingested, the quality and duration of sleep are usually affected, in addition to the fact that insulin resistance, an alteration in the release of growth hormone, different neurohormones linked to tissue recovery, and repair.

FASTING AND BRAIN FUNCTION

Fasting has a beneficial effect on the brain's level of neuronal activity. First of all, by recomposing the organism in the day/night cycles, a very positive hormonal modulation causes the dopamine levels to be high in the morning (which allows the person to be very active). The serotonin levels will remain high at night, which will be beneficial to the rest by having the lowest levels of fasting insulin, a greater release of growth hormone and more neurotrophic factor derived from the brain are permitted at night, which makes the person more neuroplastic and can prevent much better neurodegenerative pathologies like Alzheimer's, Parkinson's or multiple sclerosis. The body releases gluconeogenesis hormones (growth hormone, glucagon, cortisol and adrenaline) throughout the day by having a lower fasting blood glucose and insulin. On the contrary, people with high glucose and insulin fasting levels usually suffer from a slowdown in mental dullness and thinking.

FASTING AND DIGESTIVE SYSTEM

Fasting methods have been used since ancient times to treat all sorts of intestinal problems such as gastritis, esophagitis, gastroesophageal reflux, bowel irritable syndrome, dyspepsia, severe fermentation, etc. In the animal kingdom, we will find a curious fact that when there is a stagnant food bolus, they need to digest or have an issue with the stomach, the animals flee to fast on solid food and drink only water. This is a physiological mechanism that allows the return to equilibrium of all intestinal functions during the hours when no work is done in the digestive system.

Intermittent fasting favors that the levels of hydration in the stomach mucosa, the release of hydrochloric acid by the stomach, or the release of enzymes and bile acids return to normal during the 14-16 hours which the solid intake is not made. Similarly, we know that the intestinal flora continues to stabilize during fasting. The bacterial strains are balanced, causing some pathogenic strains not to proliferate excessively (e.g., Helicobacter pylori, candida, or other forms of intestinal pathogens). I have found benefits in fasting, ulcerative colitis, digestive systems, and irritable bowel syndrome.

FASTING AND CANCER

More and more scientists are trying to help cancer patients aim to change the oncological metabolic process to traditional treatments (chemotherapy, radiotherapy, surgery). In recent years, studies have been reported in which at the time of intermittent fasting in both animals and humans the modulating effects at the stage of metabolism were observed. Several volunteers underwent a study. The medical team discovered how glucoseinsulin levels and, most importantly, the IGF-1 values (which is a potential oncological marker) were greatly improved by fasting cardiovascular risk indicators.

INTERMITTENT FAST CONFECTION

It is focused on having enough fasting hours from the last to the first intake of the next day, distributing amounts of glucose, insulin, inhibiting the mTOR's anabolic pathway, and activating the autophagic pathway of the AMPK. It has been noted that this starts to happen after 12 hours of fasting, although the ideal is to arrive between the last meal and the first intake of the next day until 14-16 hours of fasting.

The instructions to follow depend on each person's schedules and customs, but the intermittent fasting rule, in general, suggests that after getting up there must be 3-4 hours in which no food has been consumed, thereby increasing the glucose levels. Insulin and gluconeogenesis hormones (adrenaline, norepinephrine, glucagon, growth hormone, and cortisol) will be released, t4 to t3 conversion will be favored and free testosterone bioavailability will be improved in the early morning hours. This will encourage the triggering of the autophagic route at the start of the day and mobilize the accumulated fatty acids in the visceral fat adipocytes.

Upon getting up, the first intake would be 3-4 hours. Some people take the opportunity to do their first fasting training, do it with low glucose and a lot of insulin sensitivity, which encourages a high-fat energy mobilization, with high lipolysis and induced thermogenesis because glucose is very small when training starts. One hour and a half or two hours before exercise are advised to make the first intake in other situations. To extend the activation of the AMPK route, this first intake should consist of protein and fat, particularly with medium-chain triglycerides found in coconut oil. In this way, the mitochondrial activity that works very efficiently from the medium-chain triglycerides will be very high.

Following the general guidance, carbohydrate intake should be done once the first practice is completed, thus breaking the AMPK route's function and activating the MTOR route linked to insulin receptor activation and hyperexpression. Of the body's proteins. Because of this supercompensation mechanism and improved insulin sensitivity in the previous 14-18 hours, the person can assimilate the carbohydrate much better and generate a beneficial impact through insulin, enabling him to refill better glycogen activate the routes intended for tissue formation and recovery.

Then we're going to have several more meals before we hit about 8 hours of food intake that must contain glycaemic index carbohydrates and proteins. If a person wishes to practice intermittent fasting during the seven days of the week and there are days when he does not exercise, the ideal for health purposes and to maintain insulin levels low is to reduce the amount of carbohydrate during the rest days and increase the amount of fat to have the elevated metabolic pathway of AMPK. It should be noted that fasting would not be one of the best strategies in high-performance athletes or people who eat very high calories throughout the day or are in the process of muscle hypertrophy, because in these situations you need to consume very high calories (especially carbohydrates) to have maximum glycogen levels and may cause problems at the intestinal level. Nevertheless, to boost hormonal levels and bowel functions, high-level athletes may benefit from one or two days a week of fasting.

Intermittent fasting is a technique of weight loss that involves interposing fasting periods with feeding periods. Not only "mere mortals" use this routine: athletes also use this form to remove fats that hinder their bodies.

Thanks to its simplicity, the diet is extremely popular. The approach is simply to disrupt food consumption over a certain period.

It forces the body to use its fat "reserves" to protect the biological unit. The body begins to lose weight slowly in this cycle of eating reserves.

It seems like a simple diet to do, but if you want to practice intermittent fasting, some specifics will make a difference.

A physically active lifestyle is comparable to youth's fountain: it is one of the secrets to living longer, healthier, and happier.

Stress, along with general well-being, can be controlled through physical activity, and physical activity is essential for achieving and maintaining a healthy body weight and reducing the risk of chronic diseases.

Among the benefits attributable to the practice of regular physical exercise, here are the main ones:

- It reduces stress

- It improves self-esteem, self-control, and a sense of general wellbeing

- It helps keep fit

- It helps to strengthen bones, muscles, and joints

- Increase muscle strength and endurance

- It allows to control the bodyweight

- It reduces the risk of chronic diseases (vascular diseases, some cancers, type 2 diabetes mellitus)

- It improves the regulation of blood pressure in hypertensive and glycaemic balance in diabetics

- Reduces states of anxiety and depression

Physical activity and nutrition are the two most important lifestyle variables for health. Staying active increases the amount of energy consumed, which is essential for weight control. As you age, your metabolism slows down, so you need to eat less and move more to keep your energy balance constant.

IMPLEMENTATION OF PHYSICAL ACTIVITY

Incorporating into the daily routine of a constant and moderate physical activity induces a series of physiological changes in the organism that go beyond burning calories, reducing fat, and maintaining muscle mass. In addition to promoting weight loss and improving the relationship between food and the body itself, physical activity induces a change in the body's composition and the functioning of metabolism and systems (circulatory, respiratory, etc.)

Daily physical exercise, for example, is a way to improve cardiovascular health because it acts on different fronts:

- It reduces blood pressure, favoring the control of hypertension.

- Increases the secretion of HDL cholesterol (good cholesterol), reducing the rate of blood cholesterol.

- It induces a decrease in triglyceride levels.

It decreases the production of insulin, helping to control type 2 diabetes, favoring the assimilation of nutrients, their arrival in the cells of the different tissues, and reducing the uptake and accumulation of fat.

PHYSICAL ACTIVITY

Control of cardiovascular risk factors (hypercholesterolemia, arterial hypertension, and type 2 diabetes).

- Increased lung capacity.

- Increase in muscle strength and mass.

- Increase in aerobic capacity.

- Reduction of fat mass.

It improves the person's psychological balance by inducing a state of personal satisfaction and the control of anxiety and stress.

Finally, it is worth highlighting the last benefit of physical activity. It improves the individual's relationship with food, reduces appetite, and favors the adoption of healthy eating habits.

CONDITIONS OF USE OF THE SERVICE

In no way can the information provided by this tool replace a direct health care provider, nor should it be used to determine a diagnosis, or to choose a procedure in particular cases.

WHAT ARE THE TYPES OF EXERCISES THAT ARE THE BEST FOR YOU (WOMAN OVER 50)?

It is time to set the table, but the exercises from 50 should be to get a healthy body, the following exercises work several muscles in your body as well as the buttocks and hamstrings for women over 50, create more legs stronger, thinner and with more force, to lift its rear part, the quadriceps also work, since they require that the knee be straightened with resistance.

To perform the first of these exercises, stand in front of a bench or a firm chair, place your left foot firmly on top of the bench or chair, press your left foot and push the body back until the left leg is straight, lower the body down until the right knee is flexed and repeated 10 to 15 times.

Weight balanced evenly; don't lean too far forward or too far back.

The so-called bridge exercises are not only the perfect exercise for a perfectly rounded back, but they will also help women keep their back healthy and pain-free.

DEFINE ABS FOR WOMEN

To do this great exercise called a bridge, lie down with your mouth up while on the floor, with your knees slightly bent and with your feet flat on the floor, raise your hips so that your body shapes will take a curved line from the shoulders to the knees, pause in the upper position for two or three seconds, then lower your body back to the initial position, repeat this movement 10 to 15 times, then take a short rest of five minutes maximum and repeat the number of times before recommended.

The addition of raising an arm while performing the previous exercise on the floor improves the posture and the strength of the base, which makes me feel better, it will seem more effort, but you will feel more secure.

Given the situation of reducing our belly, it is important to perform the exercises constantly and linearly; it is advisable to expand the abdominal table for women progressively, every 10 or 15 days would be correct because each time we will have the most strengthened abdominal area.

To perform the following exercise for women over 50 to create stronger, stronger legs and buttocks, start by adopting an iron position, but bend your elbows and lean on your forearms instead of on your hands.

Your body should create a straight line to the ankles from the shoulders, tighten your buttocks and maintain your hip position while raising your right arm forward, move your shoulder blades down and back as you raise your arms, keep the position for 5 to 10 seconds relax the buttocks and repeat the exercise ten to fifteen times changing arm.

There are so many physical and mental benefits with yoga, with the investment postures that are excellent to help reduce the appearance of cellulite, make shoulder support or put your legs above the wall for 5 minutes every night before going to bed, this will be beneficial not only for the appearance of cellulite but also to collaborate with its circulation greatly.

To correctly perform the following exercise after 50, you have to take it more calmly, to create stronger, more firm legs and buttocks, lie on your back and gradually lift your hips and legs off the floor, bringing your legs they will be above your head until your toes touch the ground behind you, place your hands behind your back and extend your legs stretching them in the air, creating a straight line from your shoulders to your ankles.

Keep your neck relaxed and your shoulder support hold, try to hold the position for at least one minute and then slowly reach the starting position, pause, rest, and then repeat the movement about ten more times, obviously with your respective breaks.

For a quick toning of the whole body, go through the movements described above and perform three sets of exercises about ten times or otherwise indicated by a medical condition, move as quickly as possible between the movements to the maximum calorie intake.

The next day, do other exercises, you can incorporate a few series of cardio intervals at the time of training your entire body, or you can do it separately over a longer period in these exercises for women over 50 years.

If you want to reinforce a specific part of your body, you should focus on exercises that train those particular muscles and incorporate them into your daily regimen. To continue to be effective, you should gradually increase the number of repetitions concerning how strong the muscle gets.

AN EXERCISE ROUTINE FOR WOMEN OVER 50

Multidirectional exercises help develop coordination and control while providing toning and hardening of the quadriceps, buttocks, hamstrings, and inner thighs.

To perform the following exercise, stand with your feet together, both arms stretched over your head, palms facing forward, take a wide step with your right foot towards the corner of the room at a 45-degree angle at diagonally, bending the right knee and reaching the lower part of your body in a forward motion on your right thigh, the back leg should be straight, with your heel lifted off the floor.

If you can touch the ground, do it on both sides of your right foot, lightly with your fingers, push with your right foot to return to the starting position, repeat 15 times on one leg and 15 times for the other, an option to modify This exercise is not to go so low in the stride and aim to reach with your hands at the knee or the level of the shin instead.

As quick advice, stand again out of the position described above and focus on working out the abdominals with tight buttocks, squeezing your thighs together, and maintaining good posture.

In addition to getting thinner and stronger legs, the postures that we must adapt to maintain a healthy and erect back. In addition to hardening our legs, our day to day will have a better quality of life. Now I remember what it cost to climb the stairs with a smile from ear to ear.

CHAPTER SIX

HOW THE WOMAN'S BODY CHANGES?

The body does not stop changing throughout our lives. Age and genetics are primarily responsible for these changes, although not the only ones. External factors such as tobacco, alcohol, poor diet, or excessive sunbathing are determinants for our health's deterioration over the decades.

In women's case, the number of hormones that we have determines the evolution of our body over the decades. Fertility is also key to understanding the changes that occur. Between the decades of the 20s and 60s, the woman undergoes a series of important changes, both hormonally and physically, as a result of menstrual cycles, pregnancies, and other derivatives of reproductive aging.

During this decade, the woman is full of energy and performance and enjoys a baseline health status. The body adapts to our rhythm of life and we perform better physically.

Genetics is a fundamental factor that determines endogenous aging; however, everything takes its toll. As much as at 20 years the skin is full of collagen, a weekend of excesses on the beach or smoking daily are points that accumulate against the epidermis and time. If a person with a genetic predisposition to have a thinner dermis or lighter skin, also smokes, sunbathes, and excessive gestures may have wrinkles in the 20s.

Creating good eating and exercise habits while avoiding alcohol and smoking and paying attention to eating disorders and attending gynecological exams annually.

As for the skin, during this decade and the third, the woman loses the brightness of adolescence and therefore must start using moisturizers, which should subsequently be rich in alpha-hydroxy acids.

During the second decade, the woman is in the fullness of her sexual development by ovarian activity. The secretion of hormones such as estrogen and progesterone play a fundamental role in the menstrual cycle and fertility.

At birth, our ovaries have a million oocytes and will no longer be produced. In each menstrual cycle, they are discarded, so as time progresses the possibility of becoming a mother decreases until menopause arrives. Between the ages of 15 and 25, the probability of becoming pregnant in each cycle is 40 percent. During this time, contraceptive treatments should be taken into account to avoid unwanted pregnancy and assist in the transmission of

infectious diseases.

From the age of 30, there is a decrease in metabolism, which means that we naturally burn fewer calories per minute if we do not exercise.

The specialist Concepción de Lucas points out that if you also lead a sedentary lifestyle, with work stress, or poor diet, your physical condition can worsen.

Also, this is the decade in which most Spanish women have their first child: the average is 32 years old. The expert points out that this moment is key for women. "In this decade, muscle tone is lost and, with pregnancy, the body can undergo significant changes, with increases and decreases in weight, body volume, and muscle sagging."

It is also common to observe adult acne, which usually appears in the jaw area and that is due to excessive sensitivity of the skin of that area to hormonal changes and that can be treated with oral contraceptive treatments or oral recurrences (not indicated for pregnant women since it can cause alteration is in the fetus) or synthetic, as dermatologist María Teresa Tracheole explains. This type of acne may also be due to disorders such as the polycystic ovary or the use of overly fatty cosmetics.

From the age of 30, expression wrinkles begin to appear in the areas where we are most gesturing, such as between the eyebrows or the eye area, with bags and crow's feet. The specialist recommends using moisturizers and containing active ingredients such as the alpha as mentioned earlier hydroxy acids, which seek to reshape the skin, vitamin C, and niacinamide.

You have to maintain good eating, exercise habits, and go to gynecological

exams annually, do health checks to monitor cholesterol, weight, visual, auditory acuity, and the early detection of diseases and pathologies.

From the age of 35, the woman's fertility decreases and it is increasingly difficult to get pregnant, so gynecologists advise not to delay motherhood beyond this age because, in addition to having to resort to assisted reproduction techniques, they add the risks of having abortions, hypertension, diabetes, and deformations or alterations in the fetus. From the age of 40, the probability of pregnancy in each cycle is 25 percent.

During the fourth decade of our life, a series of changes in our physiognomy begin to occur. The fat that predominated in the buttocks and legs for possible breastfeeding begins to redistribute in the abdomen, increasing cardiovascular disease risk.

Also, decrease muscle mass and tone and increases sagging in arms and legs, especially if we do not exercise.

The level of hormones drops and the woman is moving away from her period of greatest fertility.

The skin loses elasticity and sunspots begin to develop like antigens, which are more marked on the lighter skins. Expression wrinkles intensify, and facial volumes begin to vary. The expert recommends anti-spot lasers, botulinum toxin for expression wrinkles, and hyaluronic acid to treat the anogenital groove's wrinkles and volume loss.

Good eating habits and exercise will contribute to a better menopausal transition in the future, as Lucas warns. The specialist indicates that, from the age of 40, the tendency to suffer from hypertension and cholesterol, pathologies observed in men, rises.

Also, the intervertebral discs are compressed, and it is normal for spine pain, loss of muscle tone to increase, and osteoporosis or loss of bone mass. It is important that young women prevent their appearance by performing a diet rich in calcium and muscle strength exercises. This serves to condition the muscles, make them stronger and stronger. It also strengthens the union of muscle with a bone through tendons.

From 45-50 years old, women can begin to notice hot flashes, irritability,

difficulty sleeping, vaginal dryness, decreased libido, and alterations in menstruation; "We are in premenopause," explains Esparza, who advises to see it as "a natural stage in women," which must be normalized and treated if necessary, to reduce symptoms. "We must not fear it, or there are methods to prevent it, simply accept it as another stage as a person and as a woman.

From the age of 45, early menopause can also occur, which usually occurs between 50 and 55 years.

During the 50s, women begin to suffer from menopause, which is the absence of menstruation for more than 12 months and is due to the permanent cessation of follicular function. Its diagnosis is clinical and retrospective when 12 months have elapsed since the last period without any menstrual bleeding.

Lucas's conception clarifies that "there are no clear guidelines on how to deal with it because each woman has different experiences, but most of the changes in their bodies are related to it."

During this period, the alteration in the distribution of body fat continues. The appearance of the skin in terms of elasticity and hydration worsens, vaginal dryness and other mucous membranes that can cause pain during sexual intercourse are experienced, muscle tone decreases, and muscle damage deteriorates. Bones of the spine, joints, or osteoarthritis problems appear.

"It also increases cardiovascular risk, sleep and memory disorders influenced by the gradual loss of estrogen," explains the specialist, adding that lifestyle changes can cause several mood changes: "during this stage, it is normal to suffer more anxiety, depression and a decrease in mood."

In the fifth decade, the woman may also notice that she loses pubic and axillary hair and undergoes changes in hair and skin or increases in body weight.

Menopause causes that, between 50 and 60 years, the woman's skin experiences many alterations. "The decrease in estrogen that occurs at this time in the woman's life leads to a thinning of the skin and dehydration, which causes wrinkles to intensify and 'sagging' of structures.

Acclimatizing the body to the symptoms of menopause by reducing body temperature with light clothing and drinking cold drinks and exercising regularly to prevent osteoporosis. Proper nutrition, doing controlled breathing exercises, going to gynecological exams, and other medical check-ups are also tipping to keep in mind during this stage and during the sixth decade of our life.

The specialist also recalls that throughout the woman's life, the gynecologist must be present, adapting her actions to the different health and reproductive status.

At every stage of the woman, physical changes and psychological changes occur, so that the specialist must be a foothold to ask constantly. "These are vital phases that must be accepted and lived. You don't understand or doubt you have; you will have your gynecologist to solve them.

PROCESS OF THE CHANGE OF OUR BODY AND THE STATE OF WELL-BEING

Our health and well-being have taken priority in our daily lives: when we have free time, outside of work and when we are not occupied with occupations, we like to devote ourselves to activities that are healthy and fun: spending time with friends, playing sports, attending social gatherings, or participating in cultural activities, for example.

But, how do we go about attaining mental and physical well-being that will allow us to enjoy life every day and reach our full potential? We learn about new ways to promote our physical and mental health every day, but much information is still out there, and we may not have as much time as we deserve to familiarize ourselves with our health. Therefore, we are featuring a compilation of the best methods to help you feel physically and mentally healthy.

BREAK WITH A SEDENTARY LIFESTYLE

It does sound a bit cliché, but our way of life is exceptionally sedentary. At times we find ourselves suffering from the stagnation that could lead to depression because we are not taking advantage of our bodies and our surroundings (or, without going too far, to procrastinate and waste our free time, making us feel that we do not give up or take advantage of the time we have been given). Getting out into the world is an excellent way to escape this vicious cycle. This simple action could mean a considerable change in our mental state, especially for those who make it happen physically (something that always produces a feeling of health that raises our mood). Make sure you spend some time outside every day. If you spend this much time exercising in the fresh air each day, you should be able to smell the difference in your skin and hair in a few weeks. Walking is one of the healthiest exercises, and it burns the same calories as running, but it requires more effort because we walk faster. Relax and clear the mind.

TRY NEW THINGS

This may sound like an exaggeration, but every day of our lives we have the opportunity to experience new things. It is common for travelers to participate in cultural activities that enrich their travel experience. There are activities like watching plays, attending concerts and participating in cultural fairs where one can meet and learn about other cultures, explore different cultural movements of one's own country, and discover new ones.

To have a complete and healthy lifestyle, people must engage in regular exercise, whether playing sports. There are ways to improve both mental and emotional well-being. However, getting physically fit not only occurs in training but is also a way to gain benefits in other areas of life. Conducting exercise not only loosens our bodies but also exercises them, preventing them from atrophying. Another benefit of muscle growth is that it helps our physical appearance, and that, in turn, helps individuals to have a greater sense of self-confidence.

Beyond this, sport also offers a period of a shared company in the weekly routine that greatly benefits the individual. It offers opportunities for both work and play, enhancing social interaction in a very positive way. Regardless, physically fit people can practice physical exercise alone or in their home, doing various exercise routines every day. Keep in mind that physical exercise causes endorphins to be produced, which is the same as feeling happy while doing it.

NEW EXPERIENCES (EXTREME SPORTS)

You can also try out some new types of physical activities that can contribute to your workout routine while also discovering a new skill within yourself. An example is the aerial fabrics, which are in style now and can be practiced in a sports center or at home, and the wind tunnel, in which we can simulate what it is like to practice skydiving. We have in this line the type of sports where you take all of your adrenaline, and these are known as adrenaline sports. Also, you have sports like bungee jumping or any form of extreme sport that enables you to leave your stress behind and face something new.

Routines are the groundwork for a healthy life and a satisfying existence. In reality, the volume of chaos we experience hourly does not lead to greater fullness in our life, instead, it creates a fluctuating and disordered system in which our daily schedule for hunger and sleep becomes thrown off. This can lead to insomnia (a very serious problem today). It may be that a system aids thinking systematically because it encourages the standardization of daily tasks and aids in creating an organized and well-structured manner of thinking focused on a particular objective. By creating schedules and routines, we can maximize the time that we have to complete our work. This helps us accomplish our duties faster and makes it easier to cope with our stress.

Our hobbies are a representation of our personality, which means exploring our hobbies is a way of learning more about ourselves. A fantastic way to commune with ourselves every day is to regularly explore new hobbies, as well as our current ones. Doing so will also help us forge new friendships, which are a key component to maintaining our overall well-being.

To cultivate emotional and mental health, the most important point is to understand ourselves. To stay mentally and physically fit, we must allow our brain to recuperate after periods of stress or take advantage of help when we require it. Considering our problems with a mental health professional (like a psychologist) is a great way to help maintain our overall mental and emotional well-being like having a periodic physical health check-up. Alternatively, to take a step away from corporations that use up our resources and influence our daily lives for the worse, we must leave them behind to strengthen our positivity. Indeed, it is possible to improve your physical and mental health. The suggestions listed here can help you on your path to living a full life every day.

During fasting periods, the person can drink water, teas, and coffee without sugar, regardless of the strategy adopted.

Knowing what to eat in food windows is just as important as fasting since with the right food the body takes better advantage of fasting.

It is also recommended to have the assistance of a nutritionist to practice intermittent fasting, as this professional will be able to set up the best diet for you.

Below we list some foods that can be part of the menu of fasting practitioners.

- Avocado: rich in healthy fats. Studies show that adding half an avocado in between can keep the body free from hunger for a few hours straight;

- Fish: are excellent sources of protein and also healthy fats. It is recommended to consume fish at least twice a week;

- Sweet potato: it is one of the best options for those who want to do intermittent fasting, as it serves as a source of healthy fibers and carbohydrates, generating a feeling of satiety. Choose the baked or roasted version;

- Eggs: they are another source of protein, just like fish. In addition to having excellent levels of protein, they are rich in many nutrients, helping to maintain muscle mass and energy during fasting;

- Nuts and chestnuts (cashew nuts, from Pará, and others): they are great options for snacks, as they are rich in calories, proteins and also in fibers, which can contribute a lot to the feeling of satiety;

- Whole grains: they are great sources of healthy carbohydrates and fiber, they can be inserted in main meals, snacks, and breaks. Studies suggest that consuming whole grains instead of refined grains optimizes metabolism and even favors weight loss;

- Probiotics: are substances that help the intestine to function well. The yogurt, the kefir, and fermented milk foods are examples of such substances;

- Cruciferous vegetables: this group of foods includes vegetables such as broccoli, cauliflower, and brussels sprouts - all rich in fiber, a nutrient known for its ability to promote satiety for the body, in addition to contributing to intestinal health;

- Foods rich in flavonoids: A 2015 survey found that people who followed a diet rich in flavonoids decreased their BMI (body mass index) over the years.

EAT NUTRIENT-BALANCED MEALS

During feeding periods after fasting, the body must receive balanced meals in nutrients to balance metabolism. Each meal must consist of:

- Healthy carbohydrates (including fiber-rich foods like brown rice or sweet potatoes);

- Healthy proteins (lean meats like some chicken cuts, beef cuts, or fish);

- Many vegetables, beans or lentils, as well as a variety of vegetables;

- Essential fatty acids (fish, nuts, and seeds).

Also, it is important to know that intermittent fasting only has positive effects if the food eaten during meals in the feeding window contains a high nutritional value.

INCREASE YOUR CONSUMPTION OF WATER AND HEALTHY DRINKS

Water is essential for all metabolic processes, being necessary to reduce weight and body fat. It is recommended to consume at least 35 ml of water per kilogram of weight.

When the body is dehydrated, symptoms of fatigue, headaches, tiredness, among others, may appear.

Increase your intake of water, unsweetened teas, or coffee, which can also assist in metabolism activation, promoting a thermogenic effect.

The chosen foods must be healthy, avoiding processed or fatty foods as much as possible:

- Candy;

- Industrialized cookies;

- Frozen or canned foods;

- Ready sauces;

- Whole dairy products;

- Refined cereals (including rice and white bread);

- Fried snacks;

Also, it is recommended not to use too much salt and sugar in the preparation of food.

While it can be tempting to go directly into your new eating routine (the initial excitement is real), it can be difficult and make you hungrier and more uncomfortable. It is best to start slowly, doing two to three days of intermittent fasting during the first week, and then "gradually increasing week by week".

After hearing your stomach growl, it may seem like there is no way to go more than X hours without food. Understand this question: ask yourself whether hunger is boredom or real hunger. If you are bored, get distracted by another task.

If you are really hungry but don't feel weak or dizzy (which are signs that you should stop fasting as soon as possible), have a hot mint tea, as mint is known to reduce your appetite, or drink water with lemon (don't add sugar) to help fill your stomach until your next meal.

Now, if you have been trying to do intermittent fasting for some time and still feel extreme hunger between periods, you need to think about it. You need to add more nutrient- or calorie-rich foods over the eight hours or consider that this may not be the best plan for you. The addition of healthy fats, such as nut, peanut, avocado, coconut butter, and olive oil, as well as protein, during the feeding period, can help keep you satisfied and full longer.

Technically, intense hunger and fatigue should not occur when following the 16: 8 fasting method (perhaps the most common). But if you feel extremely dizzy, you are probably low on sugar and need to eat something.

By definition, fasting involves removing some, if not all, food. Your best bet? Make a protein-rich snack, like a few slices of turkey breast or one to two hard-boiled eggs (to help you stay in a ketogenic (fat-burning) state, Savage recommends. You can return to fasting, of course, if you want.

Even when fasting, drinking water and drinks such as coffee and tea (without milk) are not only allowed but especially in the case of H2O, encouraged. She recommends setting reminders throughout the day and, especially during fasting periods, to absorb lots of fluids. Try to fill at least 2, if not 3, liters per day.

After several hours without food, you can feel like a human vacuum ready to suck what's on your plate. But killing the urge in minutes is not good for your body, according to research. Instead, chew well and eat slowly to allow the digestive system to process food fully.

Just because you have stopped fasting does not mean that you should fill yourself with food. Eating cannot only make you bloated and uncomfortable, but it can also sabotage the weight loss goals that probably led you to intermittent fasting in the first place. Simply put: it's not necessarily how much of your plate can help you stay full longer, but what's on your plate.

Having a healthy mix of proteins, fibers, healthy fats and carbohydrates can help you lose pounds and avoid extreme hunger when fasting. A good example? Grilled chicken with half a small sweet potato and sautéed spinach with garlic and olive oil.

When it comes to fruits, you want to opt for those with a low glycaemic index, which is digested, absorbed, and metabolized more slowly, causing a lower and slower increase in blood glucose. A stable blood sugar level helps prevent cravings - and therefore is critical when it comes to successfully losing weight.

Although Hertz mainly recommends 16:8, you need to look at your overall lifestyle to see which fasting method can best fit. For example, if you wake up early, it may be best to eat during the early hours, such as 10 am to 6 pm, and fast until the next morning at 10 am. Remember: The beauty of fasting is that it is easily changeable and flexible to your schedule.

Another option is to stop fasting early and have breakfast every day to increase your strength gradually. We all naturally fast once a day - while we sleep - so maybe you do 'close the kitchen' early. For example, "close" the kitchen at 9 pm and don't eat again until breakfast at 8 am. This is an 11hour natural fast!

Most nutritionists do not recommend fasting for an entire day, as this can lead to increased weakness, hunger, and increased food consumption therefore weight gain.

If your goal is to lose weight, considering your total calorie intake and working to reduce that weight may be more beneficial than fasting for a long time (especially if you're the type who likes to eat afterward.)

You can exercise if you are on a fasting diet. But you have to be aware of what types of moves you make and when. If you choose to exercise on a fast, it is preferable to exercise early in the morning, when you have more energy.

Nevertheless, while you are fasting, you are not feeding your muscles properly. So, you are more likely to get hurt. Consider lower impact exercises, such as yoga or steady-state cardio, on fasting mornings, and do HIIT class after eating.

Believe it or not, keeping a food diary can help you with your fasting diet. Actively write down details such as emotions and symptoms (level of hunger, weakness, etc.) that arise during intermittent fasting. This can help you assess your progress. You can also write down any trigger points that make fasting more difficult, such as drinking the night before.

This is essential! Maintain awareness of dizziness, fatigue, irritability, headache, anxiety, and difficulty concentrating. When you have any of these situations, break your fast. This confirms that the body is in starvation mode and requires nourishment. And if you begin to feel cold, it is a sign to end the fast.

Additionally, be patient. You may feel hungrier and weaker while fasting than usual. It is okay to have these feelings for up to a week. You should abandon the diet if these difficulties last longer and if you experience similar symptoms. Do not get sick!

CHAPTER EIGHT

WHAT IS THE OMAD DIET

OMAD stands for "one meal a day" It is a form of intermittent fasting. This menu helps you prepare OMAD safely and effectively, with enough calories and protein, to help you reach your weight loss and low-carb goals.

The OMAD diet is the longest form of a limited-time window diet, equivalent to a 23: 1 fast (23 hours of fasting and ability to eat in a 1-hour time window). In its purest form, the OMAD diet does not impose a specific caloric restriction or macronutrient composition. As such, we recommend continuing the healthy low-carb diet during that meal.

When the body is in a fasting state, it uses fat reserves as fuel for energy. This leads to the breakdown and utilization of fat. This helps in maintaining lifestyle-related disorders. It also reduces inflammation levels and increases growth hormone (HGH) levels that help burn fat.

Consumption of fibrous fruits and vegetables leads to less absorption of sugar and fat in the body. Fiber also improves digestion and relieves constipation. All of these things collectively lead to weight reduction.

- OMAD diet leads to weight loss: Intermittent fasting and only 1 meal per day reduce caloric intake thus promoting weight loss.

- Useful in type II diabetes: Intake of fiber-rich foods with low glycemic index controls blood sugar spikes. Weight reduction also helps reduce hyperinsulinemia.

- Heart-friendly: Reduces visceral fat and improves heart function.

- Feeling light: Intermittent fasting reduces fat deposits in the body, making you more active and less fatigued.

- Induces self-control: The OMAD diet inculcates the habit of selecting nutritious foods. Consciously, with practice, you will overcome your cravings and overeating.

Many of those who eat an OMAD model tend to do so just for the ease of preparing food and eating once a day. This can be especially helpful for those who travel frequently, those on shifts at work, and those with busy, hectic schedules.

Think about how much time you spend shopping, planning, and preparing meals. (And let's not even talk about dirty dishes). If there are three meals a day, how much time could you save by cutting out two-thirds?

Some people see the OMAD diet as an "easy" way to reduce calorie intake. When eating is only allowed in a 30-60 minutes time period, it becomes physically difficult to exceed your daily calorie requirements.

OMAD DIET SIDE EFFECTS:

- Overeating or bingeing: When you start with OMAD, fasting for 23 hours may cause you to choose unhealthy food options. You get uncontrollable cravings for junk food and desserts. This gets better with time. As your body begins to accept the routine.

- Hypoglycemia: There is always a risk of a lack of energy. In severe cases, the person may go dark. Other symptoms include constant hunger, fatigue, shaking, inability to concentrate, and irritability. This also improves with time.

- Consistency: Calorie restriction will initially cause weight loss. But it is difficult to stick to this routine on a permanent basis. So, this may lead to weight recycling.

- Physical and Psychological Symptoms: Intermittent fasting increases stress on the body leading to anxiety-related disorders like nausea and mouth ulcers. Acidity can become a problem if your other lifestyle traits are not correct. Ex. Improper sleep and OMAD in combination can lead to acidity and reflux together.

- Sleep Disorder: Intermittent fasting and calorie restriction could affect the central nervous system. This may affect the clarity, focus, and rhythm of sleep.

- Difficult to follow: It takes willpower and fortitude to stick to this diet pattern.

OMAD is definitely not a good option for those who lack motivation and cannot resist temptation.

- Vegetables: Green leafy vegetables, carrot, broccoli, cabbage, cauliflower, red beet, lettuce, bell peppers, sweet potatoes, and squash.

- Fruits: Apple, banana, orange, grapefruit, grapes, cucumber, tomato, peach, plum, lemon, lime, pineapple, and berries.

- Animal protein: White meat such as chicken, lean meat, fish, and eggs.

- Vegetable proteins: Legumes, dal, mushrooms, soybeans, tofu, nuts, and seeds.

- Milk and its products: Whole milk, curds, cheese, buttermilk, and paneer.

- Whole grains: Brown rice, black rice, cracked wheat, millet, quinoa, and barley.

- Fats and oils: Omega-3-rich olive oil, MUFA-rich rice bran oil, sunflower butter, peanut butter, coconut oil, and almond butter.

- Nuts & Seeds: MUFA- and PUFA-rich nuts such as almonds, walnuts, pistachios, sunflower seeds, pumpkin seeds, and melon seeds.

- Herbs & Spices: Mint, fennel, thyme, oregano, garlic, ginger, onion, coriander, cumin, turmeric, pepper, cardamom, and cloves.

- Beverages: Zero-calorie beverages such as water, homemade salted lemonade, green tea, black tea, or sugar-free black coffee.

- Fruits Consume: Grapes, Jackfruit, Mango, Chikoo, Sitaphal and Pineapple in very small amounts.

- Canned foods: Canned meats, pineapples, cherries, jams, jellies or olives as it contains many preservatives, sugar, and salt.

- Milk and its products: Low-fat milk and products, flavored yogurt and cream cheese.

- Grains: with a high glycemic index such as rice and refined flour as they could lead to weight gain.

- Nuts and seeds: Limit consumption of cashews as it could also lead to weight gain.

- Fats and oils: Trans fats containing margarine, lard, vegetable oil, butter, and mayonnaise to prevent heart disease.

- Beverages: Packaged fruit and vegetable juices, carbonated drinks and energy drinks as it contains simple sugars that lead to weight gain.

TIPS OF WHAT TO DO AND NOT TO DO DURING THE OMAD DIET

WHO SHOULDN'T FOLLOW THE OMAD DIET?

- Diabetics on insulin.

- People with severe kidney or liver disease.

- Pregnant and lactating women.

- People who suffer from hyperacidity should avoid OMAD.

- Keep yourself sufficiently hydrated.

- Start by following the pattern for 1-2 days a week.

- Then gradually increase the number of days until you feel comfortable.

- You can choose the mealtime according to your convenience.

- It is important to eat at the same time every day.

- You can consume 3-4 cups of zero-calorie green tea or spiced teas during the fasting phase.

- Consume an egg or 1 serving of nuts before working out.

- Drink coconut water after your workout to replace electrolytes.

- Get at least 7 to 8 hours of sleep.

- Avoid junk foods and fruit juices.

TO FINISH ABOUT OMAD

The OMAD diet is effective in weight loss and prevents weight regain. But every individual will react differently to the OMAD diet. It will only work wonders if you change a healthy lifestyle. Always consult a qualified professional before trying anything new. The best path to a sustainable life is through a healthy and balanced diet, regular exercise, and a healthy lifestyle.

This menu helps you do OMAD safely and effectively, with enough calories and protein, to help you achieve your weight loss and low-carb goals. This plan is recommended to be used for a defined period, as it involves one meal per day (lunch or dinner). It is simple and drama-free. Plus, you'll enjoy delicious and nutritious meals. Of course, be sure to drink plenty of water (you can also have black coffee and tea). And eat enough salt to minimize side effects like headaches.

Monday Meal

🕐 5 + 10 m | beginner

Don't be shy and enjoy this classic keto breakfast for lunch or dinner. We have added walnuts and peppers to make it crisp. Why complicate things?

Ingredients:

- 70 g smoked bacon
- 2 eggs
- 1 (200 g) avocados
- 30 ml walnuts
- ½ (70 g) green bell peppers
- Salt and ground black pepper
- ½ tbsp. fresh chives, finely   chopped (optional)

<h1 style="text-align:center">At your service:</h1>

60 ml arugula

½ tbsp. olive oil

<h1 style="text-align:center">Instructions:</h1>

The steps to follow are written for 1 serving. Take this into account if you are preparing more servings.

1. Fry the bacon in butter over medium heat until crispy.

2. Remove from the pan and keep warm. Leave the accumulated fat in the pan. Lower the heat to medium-low and fry the eggs in the same skillet.

3. Place the bacon, eggs, avocado, walnuts, bell pepper and arugula on a plate.

4. Pour the remaining bacon fat over the eggs. Season to taste.

Low carb ketogenic (kcal: 937 - We do not recommend counting calories.)

Per portion:

- Net carbs: 4% (9 g)

- Fiber: 16 g

- Fat: 78% (78 g)

- Protein: 19% (42 g)

Tuesday Meal

20 + 15 m |

Medium difficulty

Cheeseburgers ... Can there be a better entree for a keto feast? They taste good and fill you up, but they are made effortlessly! And you don't need to put them on bread to dress them with delicious Mexican sauce!

Ingredients Sauce:

- ½ (55 g) tomatoes

- ½ (7.5 g) chives

- ¼ (50g) avocados

- ¼ tbsp. olive oil

- ½ tbsp. chopped fresh cilantro

- Salt to taste

Ingredients Burgers:

- 170 g ground beef (minced meat)

- 60 ml (30 g) grated cheddar cheese, divided into two parts

- ½ tsp. garlic powder ½

- tsp. onion powder

- ½ tsp. Spanish paprika

- ½ tsp. finely chopped fresh oregano

- ½ tbsp. butter, for frying

Toppings:

35 g romaine lettuce

30 ml mayonnaise

35 g cooked smoked bacon, crumbled

1 tbsp. chopped pickled jalapeños

18 g pickled gherkins, sliced

1 tbsp. Dijon mustard

Instructions:

The steps to follow are written for 1 serving. Take this into account if you are preparing more servings.

1. Chop the sauce ingredients and stir well in a small bowl. Reserve.

2. Mix the seasonings and half of the cheese with the ground beef.

3. Assemble four hamburgers and fry them in a pan or on a grill if you prefer. Add the remaining cheese on top towards the end.

4. Serve on lettuce leaves with pickles and mustard. On top, place the bacon. And don't forget about the homemade Mexican salsa!

Low carb ketogenic (kcal: 1007 - We do not recommend counting calories.)

Per portion:

- Net carbs: 3% (8 g)

- Fiber: 7 g

- Fat: 75% (82 g)

- Protein: 22% (55 g)

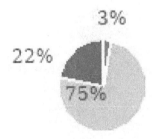

■ CARB   ■ FAT   ■ PROTEIN

Wednesday Meal

5 + 10 m | beginner

Real food on a plate. Tuna, eggs, spinach, avocado, mayonnaise, and lemon. Because a keto meal doesn't have to be complicated.

Ingredients:

- 2 eggs
- 28 g spinach sprouts
- 140 g tuna in olive oil
- ½ (100 g) avocados
- 60 ml mayonnaise /
- lemons   (optional)
- salt - pepper to taste

Instructions:

The steps to follow are written for 1 serving. Take this into account if you are preparing more servings.

1. Start by cooking the eggs. Add them carefully to boiling water and cook them for 4-8 minutes, depending on whether you like them poached or hard.

2. Chill the eggs in ice water for 1-2 minutes when done; this will make it easier to peel them off.

3. Place the eggs, spinach, tuna and avocado on a plate. Serve with a good dollop of mayonnaise and a lemon wedge if you feel like it. Season to taste.

Low carb ketogenic (kcal: 930 - We do not recommend counting calories.)

Per portion:

- Net carbs: 1% (3 g)

- Fiber: 7 g

- Fat: 76% (76 g)

- Protein: 23% (52 g)

Thursday Meal

🕐 15 + 30 m |

medium difficulty

A simple and creamy dinner. Chicken, Parmesan cheese, and the tangy touch of sun-dried tomatoes. It serves you as a normal weeknight dinner or for a weekend with friends. Serve alongside butter-fried cabbage strips instead of pasta. One more success of the keto kitchen!

Ingredients:

- ½ tbsp. butter for frying

- 170 g boneless chicken drumsticks, sliced

- 15 ml dried tomatoes in oil, finely chopped

- (35 g) cherry tomatoes cut into four pieces

- ¼ garlic cloves, finely minced

- 60 ml cream (or cream) to whip

- 75 ml (25 g) grated Parmesan cheese

- 60 ml spinach sprouts salt and pepper

-

Cabbage paste:

- 80 g shredded white cabbage

- ½ tbsp. butter for frying salt or pepper **Instructions:**

The steps to follow are written for 1 serving. Take this into account if you are preparing more servings.

1. Heat the butter in a skillet over medium heat. Fry the chicken for a couple of minutes. In this instance it is not necessary to cook it completely, since then it will continue cooking with the next ingredients. Salt and pepper.

2. Add the two types of tomatoes to the pan, along with the garlic.

3. Add the whipping cream. Let it boil over medium heat for about 5 minutes.

4. Add the grated Parmesan cheese and simmer for another 10 minutes. Season to taste.

5. Meanwhile, melt the butter over medium heat in a large skillet. Add the cabbage and fry until tender. Season to taste.

6. Spread the cabbage on serving plates. Add the spinach to the pan with the creamy chicken and stir. Finally, pour the chicken along with the creamy sauce on top of the cabbage.

Tips:

- Chicken Parmesan goes great with cauliflower rice. If you want to discover more of our garnishes, here they are all.

- You can substitute the spinach for chopped kale (without the stems).
Moderate low-Carb (kcal: 653 - We do not recommend counting calories.)

Per portion

-
-
- Protein: 29%(46g)

- Fat: 66% (48g)

Net carbs: 5% (8g)

Fiber: 3 g

5%

29%

66%

■ CARB ■ FAT ■ PROTEIN

Friday Meal

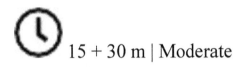 15 + 30 m | Moderate

You can add all your favorite toppings to this crispy, keto, cheese-laden pizza crust that is really going to nourish and fill you up. Bon Appetite!

Ingredients base:

- 180 ml (85 g) grated mozzarella cheese

- 90 ml (45 g) almond flour 1 tbsp. cream cheese

- ½ tsp. White wine vinegar

- ½ egg

- ¼ tsp. salt

- Olive oil to grease the hands

Ingredients on the base:

- 110 g Italian sausages

- ½ tbsp. Butter

- 60 ml tomato sauce without sugar

- ¼ tsp. Dried oregano

- 180 ml (85 g) mozzarella cheese

Instructions:

Instructions are for 1 serving. Modify them as needed

1. Preheat the oven to 200 ° C (400 ° F).

2. Heat the mozzarella and cream cheese in a small nonstick pot over medium heat or in a bowl in the microwave.

3. Mix until the mozzarella and cream cheese are melted and incorporated. Add the other ingredients and mix well.

4. Moisten your hands with olive oil and flatten the dough on parchment paper to form a circle about 20 cm (8 inches) in diameter. You can also use a rolling pin to flatten the dough between two sheets of parchment paper.

5. Remove the top sheet of parchment paper (if you used it). Prick the dough with a fork (all over the surface) and bake for 10-12 minutes until golden brown. Take out of the oven.

6. While the dough is baking, sauté the ground sausage in olive oil or butter.

7. Spread a thin layer of tomato sauce over the dough. Top with the pork and plenty of cheese. Bake for 10-15 more or until cheese has melted.

8. Sprinkle oregano on top and serve with a green salad.

Advice!

Bake additional batter and freeze for a quick and easy dinner. Or, use the extra batter to make a Rosemary Garlic Focaccia Bread – just sprinkle garlic butter on top and bake for another couple of minutes.

Low carb ketogenic (kcal: 1235 - We do not recommend counting calories.)

Half a pizza:

Net carbs: 4% (13 g)

Fiber: 1 g

Fat: 74% (100 g)

Protein: 22% (66 g)

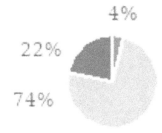

■ CARB   ■ FAT   ■ PROTEIN

KETO CHICKEN WINGS WITH CREAMY BROCCOLI

Saturday Meal

10 + 45 m | Easy

With this simple dish, you will win over the whole world! These tender chicken wings taste like glory. Combined with the creamy broccoli they are great for weeknight dinner.

Ingredients Grilled chicken wings:

- 325 g chicken wings

- / orange, juice and zest

- 15 ml olive oil

- ½ tsp. powdered ginger ¼

- tsp. salt

- / tsp. Cayenne pepper

Creamy broccoli:

- 180 g broccoli

- 60 ml mayonnaise

- 15 ml (0.6 g) chopped fresh dill

- Salt and pepper to taste

Instructions:

Instructions are for 1 serving. Modify them as needed.

1. Preheat the oven to 200 °C (400 °F).

2. Mix the orange juice and zest with the oil and spices in a small bowl. Place the chicken wings in a plastic bag and add the marinade.

3. Shake the bag well so that the wings are well bathed in the mixture. Let marinate for at least 5 minutes. If possible, allow a little more time.

4. Arrange the wings in a single layer on a greased roasting pan.

5. Bake on a wire rack in the middle of the oven for about 45 minutes or until the wings are golden brown and well done.

6. Meanwhile, cut the broccoli into small florets and boil in salted water for a couple of minutes. They should only soften a bit, without losing their shape or color.

7. Strain the broccoli and let some of the steam evaporate. Mix with the mayonnaise and dill. Season to taste.

8. Serve the broccoli along with the roasted wings.

Advice!

You can substitute broccoli for small florets of cauliflower or Brussels sprouts. If you have an outdoor grill, you can also use it to cook your wings

Low carb ketogenic (kcal: 1216 - We do not recommend counting calories.)

Per portion:

- Net Carbs: 3%(9g)

- Fiber: 5 g

- Fat: 75% (99 g)

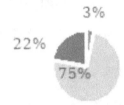

- Protein: 22%(65 g)

KETO HERB BUTTER CHEESE STEAK ROULADES

Sunday Meal

10 + 20 m |

Moderate

This is quite a keto delicacy. Tasty meat stuffed with cheese and served over leeks and mushrooms. A marvel for any night. And don't forget the herb butter, it adds a lot of aromas.

Ingredients:

- ½ leek
- 110 g mushrooms two
- thin steaks
- ½ tbsp. olive oil
- Salt and pepper
- 21 g (45 ml) cheddar cheese or gruyere cheese
- Two chopsticks
- ½ tbsp. butter for frying
- 35 g butter with herbs

Instructions:

The steps to follow are written for 1 serving. Take this into account if you are preparing more servings.

1. Trim and rinse the leeks. Cut into wide slices, using the white and green parts. Cut the mushrooms into pieces.

2. Fry the mushrooms and leeks in olive oil until they take on a good color. Season to taste. Place in a bowl and cover to keep everything warm.

3. Place the thin steaks on a large cutting board. Season to taste. Place a stick of cheese on each steak and roll. Close with a toothpick.

4. Sauté the roulades over medium heat for 10-15 minutes and reduce heat towards the end.

5. Pour the juices over the leeks and mushrooms. Serve the roulades with herb butter and the fried vegetables. Don't forget to remove the toothpick before serving!

Advice!

You can also add a pinch of chili flakes to give the leeks a spicy touch.

Low carb ketogenic (kcal: 726 - We do not recommend counting calories.)

Per portion:

- Net Carbs:3%(5g

- Fiber: 2 g

- Fat: 73% (59 g)

- Protein: 24% (44 g)

We don't recommend counting calories. First of all, it is impossible to know exactly how many calories you will get from a specific food, much less to know precisely what the body will do with those calories. It is much more important to choose foods that promote the release of hormones that reduce hunger, that help us stay full, and that make it easier to achieve a healthy weight.

We should focus on authentic foods that contain good quality protein, healthy fats, and nutrient-rich fibrous carbohydrates, especially vegetables that grow on the surface.

If you're having a hard time losing weight, refrain from high-calorie, rewarding foods - it's easy to lose control, even if they're low in carbs. Some classic examples are cheese and nuts.

Instead of counting calories, make all calories count: eat low-carb, nutritious, and balanced foods.

CHAPTER NINE

OVERCOME HUNGER ATTACKS

There are certain times of the day, of the month, or the year in which those cravings to eat anything attack us. It can be between lunch and dinner, during the menstrual period, or when it is cold. Hunger attacks appear at any time, as they are caused by different factors, such as anxiety, boredom, or hormonal changes, among others.

In general, you tend to eat processed foods, high in calories or high in sugar. When we eat food with a high glycaemic index, the blood sugar level rises more than normal. To counteract it, the pancreas produces insulin and, as a consequence, glucose drops and we are hungry again.

When the cause is related to anxiety, it can be difficult to control. Therefore, it is advisable to go to a professional to study the case individually and recommend the appropriate treatment.

TIPS TO PREVENT HUNGER ATTACKS DRINK LOTS OF FLUIDS

To avoid overeating, drink water before meals. The intake of liquid produces a feeling of satiety. That is why if you drink water, juices, or infusions before eating or when you feel like having a snack between meals, you will reduce the amount of food you eat and, consequently, the calories.

It is also a good idea to have a homemade broth as a first course, as it calms the appetite and avoids eating large quantities of the next dish.

If you suffer a glucose drop your appetite will skyrocket, so avoid it by eating frequently and keeping your blood glucose levels stable.

Breakfast is the most important meal and is fundamental to not feel hungry mid-morning.

Add whole grains, cookies, and fruit to your breakfasts. This will help the digestive system to function in optimal conditions.

It is true that if it is not cold you do not feel like eating hot food, but it should be done, even if it is warm dishes. The reason is that there are studies that show that hot foods send more signals of satiety to the brain than cold ones.

So, if you temper a dish that you were going to drink cold, you will contribute to making you feel fuller and, therefore, you will eat less.

DRIVE AWAY THE TEMPTATIONS

This is very effective advice because looking at food at all hours can unbalance your appetite.

Place chips, candy, and whatever tempts you to snack between meals in kitchen cabinets or opaque boxes. Instead, expose other lighter healthier foods like a platter full of fruit, grains, or vegetables.

EAT SLOWLY AND CHEW WELL

The feeling of fullness occurs 20 minutes after starting to eat. If you chew quickly and, in a hurry, you can eat up to two or three times more than you really need. So it is recommended, eat slowly and chew between 20 or 30 times each bite.

In this way, you will also enjoy food more, you will feel the flavors and textures on your palate, and you will avoid acidity.

According to a study from the University of Utah, there is a lag between when a person has eaten enough and when their stomach feels full. To determine the latter, the brain fixes on external elements and receives the signal to have eaten more if the plate is left empty.

For this reason, use dessert plates to 'trick' the brain into feeling full faster.

AVOID STRESS

When we have anxiety or stress, the brain stimulates the adrenal glands. These glands release cortisol, a hormone that increases motivation, including the urge to eat. Therefore, this leads you to eat more caloric foods without measure, even if you are already satiated.

To avoid reaching this situation, you must follow a balanced diet rich in foods containing vitamin B6, folic acid, and tryptophan. These nutrients promote the production of serotonin, a neurotransmitter known as the 'happiness hormone', which is involved in the proper functioning of the nervous system and also regulates appetite.

Nuts, eggs, meats, oily fish, green leafy vegetables, or bananas contain these nutrients.

Do not completely eliminate desserts from the diet because this will generate more anxiety and desire to eat. Treat yourself on time and as healthy as possible, such as an ounce or two of dark chocolate.

If you sleep fewer hours than recommended, throughout the day you will be hungrier and you will crave more caloric foods (especially sweets). It is a response of the body to compensate for the energy that has not been recovered at night, so avoid it by sleeping 8 hours a day.

Finally, it must be remembered that in case of anxiety you should go to the doctor to tell you which is the most appropriate treatment for you, be it dietary or psychological.

We can start each of the main meals (lunch and dinner) with a hearty salad to reduce hunger.

It is better to opt for dishes with more consistency, that is, they require more chewing. For example, vegetables raw instead of cooked. Thus, you will be sitting at the table for longer and eating more slowly.

It is convenient to savor each bite well and chew more times. The brain knows when the stomach is full 20 minutes after you finish eating. Also, we will enjoy the food more, we will feel the flavors and textures on your palate, we will avoid reflux or acidity, etc.

- Cut down on portions. The trick is not to stop eating certain foods, but to do so in small amounts. It is best to eat everything, but as a dessert plate, a good way to gradually reduce the amounts. Also, if you chew well and eat slowly you will increase the feeling of satiety and you will not be left hungry.

- Eat protein for breakfast. Not only are they essential for maintaining good muscle health, but they also have a satiating effect that will help control the urge to eat. Eating eggs or sausages for breakfast requires more energy to digest them and, therefore, more calories are burned, which keeps the metabolism active throughout the day.

- Join the real food. It is essential to eliminate refined flours, ultraprocessed foods, soft drinks, and sugars from the diet, replacing them with others rich in nutrients. Choose products that are not packaged and, if you do, look carefully at the ingredients on the label to avoid additives and control the amount of salt and fat.

- Cut out the sugar. It provides calories without nutritional contribution and its high intake is directly linked to weight gain, among other diseases. If you are a chronic sweet tooth, look for 0% products that do not have sugar or fat, today there are even sweets.

- Drink two liters of water daily. It is very important to regulate weight because it helps eliminate toxins and purify the body and increases energy expenditure thanks to a mechanism known as thermogenesis, which speeds up metabolism. Also, it has a satiating effect since drinking water before meals makes us feel fuller. Drink at least a liter and a half and, if it costs you, add flavor with some fruit or opt for warm infusions.

Intermittent fasting consists of alternating periods of feeding with others of fasting. Depending on the hours that we extend the time without eating, we will carry out one type of fast. The most common are 10 or 12 hours of fasting but it can also be extended to 24 hours.

According to different research, with 10 to 16 hours of fasting, the body already begins to notice the benefits of this resource, converting its fat reserves into energy and releasing ketones into the bloodstream.

It is important to include supplements that do not interfere with it or even help us make it more bearable during our fasting stage. These supplements can help us improve energy, reduce hunger and even give us a feeling of general well-being.

After getting to know the different intermittent fasting protocols and knowing how this diet can affect your body and mind, learn how to potentiate its effects through supplements. But first, an important warning: for your weight loss to be even more effective, do your workouts immediately before breaking your fast, so that right after the exercises you can eat. This strategy optimizes the recovery and synthesis of proteins and replenishes their energies.

TOP SUPPLEMENTS FOR INTERMITTENT FASTING BCAA'S

When you are in a fasted state, you cannot have anything with calories. This can be very difficult when you are having a bad day and feeling hungry. It can also cause unnecessary muscle breakdown to support the body. Enter BCAAs - the savior of both problems. Branched Chain Amino Acids will have 0 calories and will prevent muscle breakdown when consumed. They will help fill you up so you can get to your food window.

BCAAs include leucine, and since leucine suppresses muscle breakdown, a BCAA supplement helps preserve muscle while you train in a fasted state.

Why not eat protein instead, you ask? Because food will increase your insulin levels and you will no longer be fasting. Whey protein is more insulinogenic than white bread.

BCAAs, on the other hand, have less of an impact on insulin levels than food, allowing you to fast while you train. That is why many people "in the know" supplement with them before fasting exercise.

FAT BURNER

Most people who use IF choose to do so to lose weight. Do you want to amplify this process and keep your body energized? Enter a fat burner. This will help keep your mood and energy levels up while supporting MORE fat loss.

Yohimbine HCL (please ask for doctor's approval before taking it) is a strong compound that can assist with fat loss while on a fasting schedule. It is a stimulant that helps increase adrenaline and dopamine levels in the body, and this can cause an increase in alertness and feelings of well-being.

Up to 0.2 mg/kg of body weight is recommended. That means a 150 lb. person (divided by 2.2 to get kg) weighs 68kg and would work up to a dose of 14mg Yohimbine HCl or five capsules of Nutra BIO Yohimbine HCl a day.

Supplementation is most effective between meals or short-term fasting (empty stomach), you can divide the dose into 1 to 4 doses per day.

Example of other burners that you can use: Thermofield from Nutra BIO, is a complete fat burner since it also helps you control your hunger, increases energy, helps you with fatigue, and helps keep sugar levels stable a more formula simple but effective as Lipov 6 Black Ultra Concentrate.

MASS GAINERS (FOR BUILDING MUSCLE)

It becomes difficult to maintain a caloric surplus when you are on intermittent fasting. The window's purpose is to keep calories low and maximize nutrient absorption. To maximize your gains, you must consume enough calories. For a delicious, protein-rich mass gainer, look no further. Add it between meals and you will get an extra 300-900 calories for muscle-building. We suggest you take these supplements only if you do physical activity.

If you DO and you exercise in the morning, you NEED some pre. You will need that kick in the gym since you are fasting. You just have to be careful and find a pre-workout that has 0 calories.

A suitable pre-workout fasting supplement will contain (at a minimum) caffeine and beta-alanine with minimal or no sugar. May also contain coralline, L-arginine, and creatine monohydrate.

These ingredients work together to increase muscular endurance, muscle power, focus, blood flow, and performance.

It is challenging to get three meals into your window to eat. Restricting caloric intake has a similar effect as restricting meals. Missing out on essential nutrients or vitamins for muscle building is possible. Intermittent fasting and daily multivitamins are mutually beneficial.

While prolonged fasting poses an increased risk of Vitamin D deficiency, it is still something intermittent fasting should pay attention to. Vitamin D is essential for immune health and it also helps the body absorb other essential nutrients like magnesium.

An important group of nutrients that are lost during long, intermittent fasts are electrolytes. When you are in a fasted state, ketone levels in your body increase, causing insulin levels to drop and essential nutrients to be removed from the body. Although the numerous roles played by electrolytes, including sodium, magnesium, chloride, phosphate, potassium, calcium, and bicarbonate, are varied, it is essential for the nervous and muscular systems. A proper balance of electrolytes is also critical for ketogenesis, the process of converting fat into energy.

Depending on the type (s) of electrolytes missing, the symptoms of electrolyte deficiency can vary. These symptoms include:

- Nausea

- Fatigue

- Threw up

- Muscle weakness/spasms

- Headaches

- Irregular heartbeat

The possibility of low electrolyte symptoms causing a significant problem for those on a fast should be considered. An electrolyte imbalance and its symptoms can be avoided by ensuring you are giving your body enough of these essential nutrients while you are fasting.

Increasing the potassium, sodium, and magnesium levels are the most important electrolytes to supplement while on an intermittent fasting regimen. Without these three elements, which are easy to eliminate when fasting, our bodies would be deficient in the substances that maintain the

proper balance of fluids and keep our blood pressure stable.

Magnesium and probiotics

Magnesium is a mineral found in various foods such as seeds, peanuts, and milk, performs various functions in the body, such as regulating the functioning of nerves and muscles and helping to control blood sugar.

The daily recommendation for magnesium consumption is usually easily achieved when eating a balanced and varied diet, but in some cases, it may be necessary to use supplements, which must be prescribed by the doctor or nutritionist.

- Magnesium performs functions in the body such as:

- Improve physical performance, because it is important for muscle contraction;

- Prevent osteoporosis, because it helps to produce hormones that increase bone formation;

- Help to control diabetes, because it regulates the transport of sugar;

- Decrease the risk of heart disease, as it decreases the accumulation of fatty plaques in blood vessels;

- Relieve heartburn and poor digestion, especially when used in the form of magnesium hydroxide;

- Control blood pressure, especially in pregnant women at risk for eclampsia.

In addition, magnesium is also used in laxative medications to fight constipation and in medications that act as antacids for the stomach.

MAGNESIUM-RICH FOODS

Foods rich in magnesium are usually also high in fiber, with the main ones being whole grains, legumes, and vegetables. See the full list:

- Legumes, such as beans and lentils;

- Whole grains, such as oats, whole wheat, and brown rice;

- Fruits, such as avocado, banana, and kiwi;

- Vegetables, especially broccoli, pumpkin, and green leaves, such as kale and spinach;

- Seeds, especially the pumpkin and sunflower seeds;

- Oilseeds, such as almonds, hazelnuts, Brazil nuts, cashew nuts, peanuts;

- Milk, yogurt, and other derivatives;

- Others: coffee, meat, and chocolate.

MAGNESIUM SUPPLEMENTS

Magnesium supplements are usually recommended in cases of deficiency of this mineral, being possible to use both a multivitamin supplement in general containing magnesium and the magnesium supplement, which is normally used in the form of chelated magnesium, magnesium aspartate, magnesium citrate, magnesium lactate, or magnesium chloride.

Supplementation should be indicated by the doctor or nutritionist, as the recommended dose depends on the cause that is causing your deficiency, in addition, its excess can cause nausea, vomiting, hypotension, drowsiness, double vision, and weakness.

PROBIOTICS

Probiotics are foods or supplements that contain live microorganisms intended to maintain or enhance the "good" bacteria (normal microbiota) in the body. Prebiotics are foods (generally high in fiber) that act as nutrients for the human microbiota. Prebiotics are used with the intention of improving the balance of these microorganisms.

Probiotics are found in foods like yogurt and sauerkraut. Prebiotics are found in foods like whole grains, bananas, green leafy vegetables, onions, garlic, soybeans, and artichokes. Additionally, probiotics and prebiotics are added to some foods and are available as dietary supplements.

The gut microbiota's connection to disease is being researched. The health benefits of probiotics and prebiotics currently available have not been proven conclusively.

However, side effects are uncommon, and most healthy adults can safely consume prebiotics and probiotics-containing foods. Future research could lead to more advanced probiotics with greater health benefits.

To get the most out of your 50s, you have to keep upping your nutrient intake as you age. Once a person's body has finished going through certain changes, a series of important events occur in their bodily system, which influences many vital organs' functioning. It is critical to follow a healthy diet to help prevent the development of chronic illnesses.

Whether or not you already know this, I think you should know that dietary requirements change with age and lifestyle. Athletes, for example, require a higher level of carbohydrates than people who are not involved in regular physical activity. Just as is the case with nutritional needs in general, the amount of nutrients required through diet differs depending on the individual's age.

Once you have discovered the nutrients you should be concerned about, you will find out which of those nutrients are crucial in your diet because of their health effects. But if you do have any questions, please consult your trusted nutritionist.

CALCIUM

A calcium deficiency can lead to bone problems. It has been shown to help prevent bone fractures. These things age you, which is why you should keep ingesting them.

However, this nutrient is much more important in women than in men. This is because, after menopause, they are more likely to develop osteoporosis due to hormonal changes.

On the other hand, it is necessary to ensure that vitamin D levels are adequate. This substance plays a key role in allowing calcium to be absorbed at the intestinal level, where it then makes its way to the bone tissue where it must carry out its essential functions.

Vitamin B12 is essential in the differentiation of red blood cell lines. Anemia occurs without this compound, causing extreme fatigue and tiredness. According to a study in the Medical Clinics of North America, "megaloblastic anemia" was once known as "metaphosphate osteodystrophy".

Developing a disease like this could have a significant impact on lifestyle habits. To ensure that the requirements are met, simply include animalbased foods in the diet regularly.

It has been commonly claimed that high-protein diets are bad for the liver and kidneys. However, current evidence disputes this.

Some nutrients must be increased in the diet by the age of 50 to preserve lean mass, as suggested by research. A daily protein intake of 1.4 grams per kilogram of bodyweight might be ideal.

Remember that the ingested proteins must be 50% of high biological value. All essential amino acids and a good digestibility value must be present. Also, those who are from animal-based foods exhibit both characteristics

It is necessary to highlight certain foods in the diet to avoid deficiencies that may negatively affect health.

The taste for meat and fish does diminish after age, and the preference for these meats wanes as one gets older, but it is imperative to keep up a consistent diet of meat and fish to maintain proper nutrition. These products contain high-quality proteins and essential micronutrients, like iron, that can avoid the risk of anemia.

Eggs and cholesterol were once believed to increase cholesterol and raise LDL (bad cholesterol) levels, but now the myth has been debunked. Even if these foods may not influence the body's lipid profile or the risk of cardiovascular disease, they appear not negatively to influence cardiovascular disease risk.

Also, they supply amino acids and fats which help with promoting a healthy state of well-being. Finally, they have vitamin D, a nutrient that is severely lacking in a large segment of the population. It is recommended that you consume at least 5 servings of it each week.

Leafy green vegetables are known to contain phytonutrients and vitamin C in their composition. While each element is required for proper bodily functions, it is equally important to ensure proper bodily reactions each day.

It should be noted that this vitamin is an essential nutrient that keeps the immune system in an operational state and thus keeps different infectious diseases at bay.

You can still include foods as you age; however, other health strategies to consider, such as increasing the frequency of consumption or choosing specific foods to increase intake.

Fasting has been proven to improve insulin resistance and reduce fat levels in those who follow it. Most people can benefit from them, though they are not ideal for everyone. To be sure, consulting with a professional is always a good idea.

Melatonin is a neurohormone synthesized in the pineal gland and regulating sleep-wake cycles. From the age of 50, its production drops dramatically, which can condition the quality of rest.

To avoid having the condition, you should ingest it externally. Consumption of 1.8 milligrams of the substance 30 minutes before going to sleep helps reduce the number of interruptions that happen during the night. Additionally, it is a powerful antioxidant, which has beneficial effects on the promotion of pathologies comprised of several factors.

The intestinal microbiota undergoes a variety of changes as the years go by. The change in the diversity of species that occurs over time may alter digestive function.

Thus, it is essential to consume fermented dairy, such as yogurt or kefir regularly. The good bacteria found in these foods are capable of colonizing different areas of the digestive tract, and as a result, they can benefit the host's overall health.

CHAPTER ELEVEN

INTERMITTENT FASTING AND GOOD HABITS

A good breakfast is essential for beginning the day on the right foot and having the needed energy to handle everything. How many times have we heard the importance of breakfast been preached to us? Despite that, we simply cannot eat anything. We wake up without an appetite, or in a hurry, so we do not even have the time to eat anything. This is a significant blunder.

Professionals never tire of repeating the importance of not skipping breakfast. You must remember, first of all, that you have not eaten anything in many hours, and the body needs to replenish energy. It seems contradictory, but people who eat a good breakfast have fewer weight problems and those who do not have problems with memory and concentration problems and, of course, have a bad character throughout the day.

THE IMPORTANCE OF BREAKFAST: HAVE A GOOD BREAKFAST AND START THE DAY STRONG

Breakfast represents the breaking of the fast, lays the foundations of a good diet, and benefits health. Thanks to breakfast, the body can stay strong, with higher concentration and energy levels throughout the morning.

In the case of children, the importance of breakfast is even greater, of course. Your body and brain are in full growth and are highly dependent on regular food consumption. By skipping breakfast and going for a long period without eating, the child could suffer from various physical, intellectual, and behavioral problems.

However, we often skip this meal, because we are in a hurry, out of laziness, or because of the false idea that by skipping breakfast, one can lose weight more quickly. However, a study cited in Pediatrics found that teens who ate breakfast daily had lower body mass index than teens who never ate breakfast or ate breakfast only occasionally.

WHAT CAN A BALANCED BREAKFAST INCLUDE?

- Dairy products. You can choose the ones you like the most, but it is better if they are whole. Mainly milk or yogurt is ideal. They provide vitamins, proteins, and calcium.

- Fruits. It is a basic element, if you also take them with skin, they give you the fiber you need. They also contain minerals, carbohydrates, and vitamins. Keep in mind that fiber has been shown to increase feelings of fullness.

- Cereals or whole wheat bread. They have not only carbohydrates from which to draw energy but also fiber.

- Eggs.

- Meat, for example, ham. But be careful, it is not advisable to overdo this ingredient.

- Coffee or herbal teas.

It is important to keep in mind that breakfast should provide about 25% of your daily caloric intake. Of course, we must try to combine the different elements in a balanced way, so that the body can absorb the necessary vitamins, fiber, carbohydrates, and minerals.

AVOID TRANS FATS AT BREAKFAST

One of the main problems in the breakfast of many people is unhealthy products, high in simple sugars and trans fats. This class of elements is capable of increasing inflammation in the body and the chances of getting sick.

Therefore, when planning a breakfast, you must include quality food, such as the ones we have mentioned. This way, you will make sure to carry out an adequate supply of nutrients to guarantee the body's proper functioning during the day.

Anyway, suppose you have doubts about making a good breakfast. In that case, what products to include or how to distribute them throughout the week, it is best to consult a professional or nutritionist.

A professional in the field can help you find a good, healthy, and balanced diet. This way, you will maximize the benefits of taking care of the first meal of the day.

Losing or gaining weight is not just about eating healthier, but also about the times when it is done. Although it is not about following a strict schedule, except in diets prescribed by specialists, there are fundamental rules when eating certain foods.

Next, we will see some recommendations on the most appropriate times to take each food. Chrono nutrition is the science that studies the effects of nutrients depending on when they are consumed. This discipline is set to gain a lot of importance in the coming years.

Today, most specialists argue that people should eat at least five times each day. That includes the traditional breakfast, lunch, and dinner, plus two snacks or snacks, between meals.

This is complemented by another idea that seems to be quite ingrained within the medical profession. They argue that the periods between one meal and another should not exceed three hours. On the contrary, overweight problems may appear or it may be difficult for us to lose the excess kilos.

The reason for this statement is that, once this time has passed, the body will notice that it is not receiving enough energy recharges and will start saving. This could cause your metabolism to slow down and not burn calories properly.

However, the most current trends are beginning to see other possibilities. One of them is intermittent fasting protocols, which are effective in improving body composition.

The first meal of the day has to be used to replenish all the energy used during the hours of sleep. Also, it also prepares the body for the day of physical and mental effort that is about to start.

Specialists recommend not skipping any meal and in the case of breakfast, it is essential. You have to start the day by taking the necessary nutrients.

It is understood that the healthiest breakfast consists of dairy food, fruit, and cereals. However, this is not a closed rule, it depends on each person. The important thing is that it is as healthy as possible. As for the schedules, you should have breakfast as early as possible. It is best not to do it after 10.

Some specialists maintain that the best time to eat the "third" (not the "second") meal of the day is between 1:00 and 3:00 p.m.

Eating high-calorie meals after 3 p.m. can be particularly counterproductive. This is because the process of digesting food becomes more inefficient so you could gain more weight. The latest research suggests that eating too early may reduce the risk of gaining fat mass.

Just as breakfast should be forceful to gather energy for the day to begin, dinner should be the lightest of all meals of the day.

It is healthier to have an early dinner to give your body time to digest. Also, fish or lean meats are recommended, accompanied by some dairy (as long as we do not have gastric problems.)

Food intakes after 10 pm can make us gain a little more weight and, also, cause nightmares and insomnia problems.

Desserts are usually always in the spotlight when talking about diets, losing weight, or not gaining weight.

Some assure that they should be banished from the menu without any contemplation.

There are fewer radical opinions, which argue that they can be eaten in moderation. However, in no case, after any of the three main meals.

In the case of desserts, it is recommended to take them first thing in the morning, since before noon the body processes carbohydrates much better.

Another good time is just before starting any physical activity. Thus, you will fill the body with energy, without forcing the stomach too much.

One tip that is becoming fashionable is to have a piece of fruit before eating and not as a dessert. This can be a good way to decrease hunger and feeling.

Besides, to achieve a satiating effect.

HYDRATION WELL: AS IMPORTANT AS EATING

There is no healthy diet if you don't consume enough water. This helps us feel more satiated, which can help us lose weight. Besides, it also contributes in a certain way to the metabolism of fats.

Specialists also recommend certain times for this:

- Two glasses of water as soon as you wake up to cleanse the body.

- A glass half an hour before the main meals, as well as before bathing and sleeping.

In total, you should consume between a litter and a half and two liters of water a day. However, these schedules alone do not work. We must combine them with a balanced diet and regular exercise.

It is generally known that sugary foods are a significant contributor to obesity. Conversely, since they increase the risk of diabetes, obesity, and heart disease, they also cause them.

- Replace refined sugar with healthy sweeteners like honey or stevia.

- Read the labels of the foods you buy at the grocery store and make sure they are low in sugar and saturated fat.

- Calm your sweet tooth with "light" desserts or nuts.

Not eating a good breakfast everyday makes it difficult to regain your ideal weight. Not only have those who avoid the food run the risk of being overweight, but their physical and mental well-being also suffer.

- Make sure you prepare a complete and balanced breakfast, which

corresponds to 25% of your total daily calories.

- Eat plenty of fruits, vegetables, and complex carbohydrate sources.

- Don't forget a small helping of healthy fats and protein.

There are many ways in which water helps to improve your figure and body weight. Since much of the body is made up of this fluid, it is essential for metabolism and an optimal detoxification process.

- Drink between 3 and 4 liters of water a day.

- If you do not want to drink only water, supplement your fluid intake with herbal teas, natural juices, or fruits rich in water.

- On hot days or when doing sports activities, increase your consumption.

To successfully lose weight, ensure that you do not skip any rest days. Despite appearing to be unrelated, sleep plays a central role in metabolic functions and all weight-loss-related processes.

- Try to sleep without interruptions for 7 or 8 hours a day.

- Avoid distractions before sleeping so as not to shorten the rest period.

- Light dinner so that you do not have digestive discomfort when going to bed.

Reducing carbohydrate consumption has interesting effects in controlling overweight. However, it is not advisable to eliminate them from the diet. These macronutrients are a major source of energy that should be incorporated into any meal plan.

- Instead of choosing simple carbohydrates (bread, pastries, flours, etc.) opt for complex carbohydrate sources (oatmeal, brown rice, quinoa, etc.)

- Try to consume them only for breakfast and lunch.

Large plates are not a good option for a healthy and slimming diet. While they are satisfying for the moment, they overload digestion and slow metabolism. The best option is to divide the servings by five or six meals a day.

- Eat small meals every 3-4 hours.

- Choose to have 3 main meals and 2 snacks.

To return to your ideal weight, you must avoid salt. Although this condiment is commonly used in the kitchen, overconsumption negatively affects both health and figure. Too much salt causes high blood pressure, inflammation, and fluid retention.

- Use herbs and spices to enhance the flavor.

- Do not use your favorite products if they contain a lot of sodium.

Regular physical exercise is the best complement to your diet. This type of activity starts the metabolism and optimizes the energy burn. Therefore, following a training routine or playing sports is very beneficial.

There are many intermittent advantages of fasting that scientists have found to reduce caloric intake for one cause or another. Intermittent fasting is described as some fifteen hours without eating. With this approach, the body will adjust several characteristics for the better. The real question is not if fasting can help you or not, but how it will help you and how often you should.

This fasting style has been shown to lower blood pressure and increase levels of HDL. It can help greatly with diabetes management and will also help you lose weight. All these effects sound pretty good and can be achieved with the fasting of this type. Studies carried out on several different animal species show that limiting caloric intake increases their lives by 30 percent.

Human studies show it reduces blood pressure, blood sugar, and sensitivity to insulin. With these experiments, fasting would improve a human's life if performed for an extended period. Cutting the calories by 30 percent all the time will achieve the same results, but this has been shown to cause depression and irritability. Fasting is a method offered instead of simply cutting calories and it has benefits without stress or irritability.

Intermittent fasting works out every other day by eating food. You will end up eating nearly twice as much food on the days you eat as you normally would. You still get the same number of calories but you are also getting all the benefits. It will lower the levels of stress and improve your overall health. This kind of fasting is a great way of getting into better physical condition, living a longer life, and feeling better all the time.

There is a strong relationship between stress and our body. For example, muscle tension is a reflex reaction to stress; it is the body's way of protecting itself against danger. It may feel like a little ache or something tightening in the back of your neck or lower back as you type on the computer. Headaches are a close cousin. The relationship is so strong that it has its term: stress headaches (also known as "tension pains.")

Stress even causes digestive problems as it alters the concentration of acid in the stomach that can lead to inflammation, colic, diarrhea, constipation, irritable bowel syndrome, and even peptic ulcers. Stress disrupts the body's insulin production, which can lead to diabetes and even heart attacks or strokes. Healthy diets have been shown to prevent these damaging physical effects of stress and even reverse the ageing process. Life is short, and your diet is an easy way to take control and maximize your well-being.

Eating a healthy diet will make you a more effective leader. You owe it to yourself to properly feed your body and brain, so here are four steps to creating a successful eating plan.

GIVE PRIORITY TO BREAKFAST

Starting the day well is important. You should get into the habit of eating breakfast. Skipping breakfast can make it difficult to maintain stable blood sugar levels. What you give to your body is also important. Try to choose foods high in fiber like cereals, oatmeal, whole wheat bread, and fresh fruit. High-fiber foods digest more slowly and keep you satisfied, as well as jump-start your metabolism and stabilize your blood sugar levels, allowing you to focus and reduce your anxiety and stress.

As a leader, breakfast may be the most important meal of the day, but it doesn't end there. Intermittent fasting for sugar control and weight loss can harm your mind and the relationships you have with your team. When you value the connection between your stomach and your mind, you get the most out of your day. The gift that is life is quite short and fleeting.

LIMIT THE CONSUMPTION OF REFINED SUGARS AND PROCESSED FOODS

Certain foods can harm your brain. Do not go near refined sugar. White sugar and high fructose corn syrup should be avoided. You should not give your team these foods, as you want them to be successful too.

Low-sugar diets have been shown to increase brain neurotrophic factor (BDNF), a peptide responsible for creating new neurons. This peptide makes neurons connect and combine, in addition to playing a fundamental role in neuroplasticity.

Try to avoid filling your kitchen with products high in sugar and foods with a high glycaemic index such as bread, sweet drinks, and fast food. Better try fruit, honey, or maple syrup. Or better yet, go for a natural protein like soy that will help you build muscle. Refined sugars will give you a quick energy boost, but you'll soon feel like your blood sugar is on a roller coaster ride, not a fun one.

When sugar levels drop, your adrenal glands release stress hormones like cortisol. This will affect your performance as a leader. You will be more irritable in conversations; your relationships will suffer and you will not make the correct decisions that your team needs.

INCLUDES OMEGA-3 FATTY ACIDS

Omega-3 fatty acids are gifts for any leader and you deserve to include them in your diet. Nuts and seeds, including chia, flaxseed, and walnuts, are your best friends and partners. Nuts are known to protect the heart and contain antioxidants. Walnuts are particularly healthy and a rich source of omega-3 fatty acids that reduce the risk of heart attacks and bad cholesterol.

Omega-3 helps stabilize adrenal hormones and prevent them from spiking, especially when you're stressed, thus becoming a powerful antidote to stress.

Craving caffeinated foods is natural. We all crave coffee, tea, soda, or chocolate, but it's important to recognize that these foods can affect our overall well-being. Caffeine stimulates the production of cortisol, the stress hormone. Having an occasional cup of coffee is fine, but try to avoid it before bed because it can give you insomnia. You should also think about when and how to consume alcohol. Alcohol is a depressant and sedative that alters neurotransmitters in the brain. Having a couple of beers or a couple of glasses of wine after work may sound tempting, but try not to overdo this habit because it could negatively affect your performance as a leader.

When you are stressed, it is easier to indulge in cravings and give in to impulses, facilitating drug or alcohol use as a defense mechanism. In the long term, this can result in addiction. It is best to avoid these temptations when you are experiencing high levels of stress.

You're eating habits and the level of stress you handle go hand in hand. When you're stressed, it's natural to crave comfort foods like desserts, fast food, and alcohol, but these foods can be addictive and wind you down a dead-end spiral. Fuelling your body for success will reduce stress, improve your productivity, and strengthen your relationship with your team, so keep these four steps in mind to create a high-performance eating plan.

TIPS TO START A HEALTHY LIFE

- Learn something new every day. Healthy entrepreneurs are eternal dreamers: They work hard, play hard and think hard. They love to read, listen to audiobooks, and absorb as much knowledge as possible. They educate themselves on topics relevant to their business, they also seek knowledge of other types. They know that healthy behaviors have a direct impact on their business.

- Set goals and create systems to achieve them: Healthy entrepreneurs also understand that knowledge without application is the fastest path to failure. They go beyond learning - they apply. They realize that daily journeys and steps are the only way to achieve goals.

- If you want to make the most of your free time, spend it wisely: It is estimated that the average person spends three hours per day watching television. That is a very kind thing of you to do, but please do not be that kind of person. To stay healthy, you should concentrate on growing your business, taking care of yourself and your family, and making the world a better place. Another piece of advice is to spend time or engage in meditation to gain a better sense of your goals.

- Make exercise a priority. A healthy body helps cultivate a healthy mind: An adult should exercise 2.5 hours a week or more with moderate to intense aerobic activity and two intensive training sessions a week. Even if you are very busy, find 10 minutes here and there. Doing so will help you relieve stress and get endorphins to overcome your business challenges.

- Eat less junk food. Think of food as fuel: The higher the quality of fuel you put in your tank, the better you will perform. You don't need to go on a diet to eat healthily. Only eat more real foods (that come from nature), instead of processed and fast food. Doing so will improve your energy level and mood, among other benefits.

- Get more sleep. All entrepreneurs experience sleepless nights, morning meetings, and last-minute deliveries. But a healthy entrepreneur knows that sleep is essential to their success. Whether you're getting up early and getting big projects done in the morning or you're hopelessly awake, find a consistent sleep routine and stick with it. Don't underestimate the power of a good nap to recharge your brain, either.

- Create a balance in your life: Healthy entrepreneurs treat their health as a lifestyle. You can't put a Band-Aid on a bad Business Plan, just like you can't eat healthy for a week and hope to lose weight. Successful entrepreneurs adopt a healthy lifestyle: They work smart, they don't work anymore.

CHAPTER TWELVE

MYTHS ABOUT INTERMITTENT FASTING

There are many myths about intermittent fasting, let's talk about the most typical, especially concerning fitness.

If you want to gain muscle mass in the world of fitness, you have to make many meals to accelerate the metabolism, incorporate protein in each of them, and do not forget to drink your post-workout shake.

Of course, many fitness gurus will never recommend you perform fasting workouts for the possible loss of muscle mass, so let's shed some light on it.

In general, there is an excessive and irrational fear that our metabolism will slow down. In this book on the reverse diet and metabolic tomb, we have already seen the real impact of caloric restriction and weight loss on metabolism.

Performing fasting periods does not reduce our basal metabolism, yes, it has been repeated throughout life that if you skip breakfast your metabolism is reduced, your body goes into saving mode and you will accumulate body fat.

But this statement is false, skipping breakfast does not reduce metabolism.

On the other hand, in several studies, it has been observed that fasting does not reduce metabolism either. In fact, in this study it was observed that fasting increased the levels of norepinephrine, a catecholamine with different physiological functions, increasing metabolism.

Another reason for criticizing intermittent fasting is the frequency of meals.

Some people say that intermittent fasting is not a good option to lose body fat because the number of made meals is reduced, which can hurt metabolism.

We know that there is no difference between making 3 or 6 meals when losing body fat. This study also reaches the same conclusion, making more meals a day does not translate into a greater loss of body fat.

On the other hand, some studies conclude that alternating fasting days is more effective for losing weight than traditional caloric restriction. In contrast, in others, it has been observed that it is not superior after one year of follow-up.

The nutritional strategy to follow depends on the person, as always you have to individualize, and some people will adapt better to fasting so that the results will be better.

But it must be made clear that fasting does not reduce metabolism, in any case, the short-term impact would be positive.

FASTING CAUSES LOSS OF MUSCLE MASS

The fasting not only reduces your basal metabolism but also makes you lose muscle mass as many keep repeating today.

Although caloric restriction (especially if the caloric deficit is very aggressive) can lead to a loss of muscle mass, this loss of muscle mass will be greatly reduced if we include strength training and enough protein in the diet.

If we add the fast to this equation, the result remains the same. If you perform heavy strength workouts, include enough protein in your diet, and control the calories you are consuming, the loss of muscle mass will be minimal.

In different studies, it has been observed that it is possible to lose body fat and maintain muscle mass while following a fasting protocol.

It has been observed that in people who practice Ramadan (with experience in training) there is a loss of body weight, but not muscle tissue.

FASTING INCREASES THE FEELING OF HUNGER SO THAT YOU WILL EAT MORE

In many studies, there has been an increase in the feeling of hunger.

That is, in general, fasting does seem to increase the sensation of hunger. Still, it has not been observed that this contributes to an increase in caloric intake throughout the day the opposite has been observed, performing 1 day of fasting translates into a 30% reduction in caloric intake the next 3 days, 30%.

Besides, under my personal experience, there is a period of adaptation, the feeling of hunger is reduced as you practice more intermittent fasting, my recommendation is that while you do it try to be active and do things, some exercise is fine, although if you are starting it is better to start progressively.

Another of the supposed benefits is that performing fasting workouts improves athletic performance.

The reality is that there is no scientific evidence to affirm that fasting improves athletic performance. The studies available today contradict this claim, training on an empty stomach is not a strategy Useful to improve performance.

In fact, and it is important to mention it, in these studies, the maximum that is achieved is to maintain the performance, and not always since in several of the sports performance is reduced (although it could be due to other factors).

MYTH 1: YOUR METABOLISM SLOWS DOWN

This idea has its origin in studies with mice, but there are two problems:

A mouse has a short life (2-3 years). A fast of a day in a mouse would perhaps equal more than a week in a human.

Mice have very little fat and are more sensitive to caloric deficits. On the contrary, humans are mammals with more% fat.

Interestingly, in us, fasting causes a slight increase in metabolism, partly because of the release of norepinephrine and orexin. It is an evolutionary adaptation: motivation to go hunting.

Of course, a prolonged fast will slow the metabolism. It is logical, knowing that leptin takes several days to reduce enough hypothalamus to react, regulating downward energy expenditure.

As we saw in this book, what slows down the metabolism is precisely a prolonged period of a hypocaloric diet, just what they recommend.

MYTH 2: BURN MUSCLE

When your body has consumed all the amino acids in the blood and stored glycogen, start using protein stores, your muscles, to convert them into glucose (via gluconeogenesis). You should avoid this process, but fortunately, it does not happen in the first 24 hours of fasting. A couple of examples:

This study concludes that intermittent fasting retains more muscle mass than a traditional hypocaloric approach (with similar fat loss).

Another study with intermittent fasting in obese adults finds that it is effective for weight loss, even increasing muscle mass. This study also compared intermittent fasting with a high-fat approach (45% of total calories) against another moderate in fat (25% of total calories). The high fat achieved greater muscle gain and fat loss. Interesting.

One possible limitation of these studies is that they are performed in overweight people, and we know that fat protects the muscle.

What would happen in people with a lot of muscle and low fat?

According to this study in Muslim bodybuilders, fasting during the month of Ramadan does not result in loss of muscle mass. Women who trained strength with intermittent fasting (16/8) gained the same amount of muscle as those who did more meals, but I lost some more fat.

It may be due in part to the increase in growth hormone generated by fasting, the protective role of autophagy, and the reduction of myostatin, which inhibits muscle development.

Supplement companies invest a lot of money in promoting the need to ingest 20g of protein every 3 hours not to catabolize. His dream would be for everyone to drink protein shakes on snacks. It is not necessary.

But more is not better, a prolonged fast is dangerous for the muscle. Your tolerance level will depend on the accumulated glycogen and physical activity performed, but in general, I do not recommend frequent fasting for more than 24-36 hours. Run away from detox diets for a week, for example.

The body is designed to maintain the proper level of blood glucose. When you eat you produce insulin to store excess glucose? When you fast you produce glucagon to release stored glucose? Eating frequently to control blood glucose externally is not necessary. You can dedicate your time to more productive things.

Intermittent fasting helps restore sensitivity to a greater extent than classical calorie restriction in people with insulin resistance.

In another study, people with type II diabetes responded better to two large meals a day than six small ones. We also know that intermittent fasting is effective against metabolic problems.

The impact of fasting on performance depends on many factors, such as the type of physical activity, the duration of fasting, and the level of adaptation. Still, there are many examples where this loss of performance does not materialize, once adopted.

Reviews of studies in Muslim athletes during Ramadan show inconsistent results. Resistance tests are most affected, but it is necessary to consider that during Ramadan the fluids are also restricted during the day, so it is difficult to know what effect is due to fasting and which is due to daily dehydration. In any case, the variations are small.

The truth is that fasting training (with low glycogen) favors adaptations that would not occur if you always train with full reserves. Here I talk more about the subject.

And finally, a recent study in strength athletes demonstrates that an intermittent fasting strategy not only maintains muscle performance and gains but is more effective in losing fat. The same concludes this study in women.

It is possible that all this happens, the first time. Like everything, it is a matter of adaptation.

But there is much evidence against distributing food in many small intakes:

This study concludes that increasing the frequency of meals increases hunger.

Another study suggests that it can promote a higher caloric intake.

My experience: the most important thing to improve adherence (and therefore success) is to be satiated when you eat. If you eat 1,800 calories a day and divide it into 6 intakes, you have 300 calories left over. Result: constant hunger. This study finds that compressing the feeding window reduces appetite.

Regarding irritation, it is subjective, but some studies indicate that intermittent fasting improves mood and symptoms of depression and improves mental alertness.

Personally, it would irritate me much more to have to prepare six meals a day and never be satiated. Intermittent fasting represents great mental and time release.

YOU WILL GAIN WEIGHT

Simply absurd. Multiple studies show that intermittent fasting helps you lose fat, better overall than classic hypocaloric diets. Recent reviews already recognize it as an effective strategy to lose weight.

The justification of some is that by skipping one meal you will accumulate hunger and you will eat twice as much at the next meal, but we know that does not happen.

CONCLUSION

Even a single human fasting cycle (e.g., overnight) will reduce the basal concentrations of many chronic disease-associated metabolic biomarkers, such as insulin and glucose. For example, for many metabolic substrates and hormones, patients need to fast for 8–12 hours before the blood draws to steady-state fasting levels. An important clinical and science issue is whether it is a viable and effective population-based approach to improve metabolic health to follow a normal, intermittent fasting regimen.

Also, intermittent fasting schemes aim to turn the positive effects of fasting schemes in rodents and other animals into realistic eating habits to reduce the risk of chronic disease in humans. In the section on Future Issues, we discuss issues that should be answered in research into intermittent fasting and metabolic health.

This summary indicates that intermittent fasting schemes can be a positive solution to weight loss and metabolic health change for people who can comfortably manage periods of not eating or eating very little for several hours of the day, night, or weekdays. If proven to be effective, these eating regimes can deliver positive, non-pharmacological solutions to populationlevel health improvement with multiple benefits for public health.

HOW INTERMITTENT FASTING HAS CHANGED ME?

My intermittent fasting experience is very good, otherwise, I would not have kept it (and still do) for so long. Personally, it has given me very good results both in body composition and improving my relationship with food. Of course, those results come over time, when it's part of your lifestyle they aren't overnight changes.

If we talk about body composition, intermittent fasting added to training (especially strength training,) and a healthy diet, it has allowed me to maintain a good muscle mass level and reduce my percentage of body fat. In the times when I have strictly followed training and nutrition, I have managed to go down to approximately 16.5%; But, more importantly, in times when I have to reduce workouts for any issue, I have stayed without problems at around 20% without much effort and maintaining a good base of lean mass.

Regarding the relationship with food, intermittent fasting has helped me to notably reduce my anxiety when it comes to eating: knowing that I have established times to eat and that, within them, I eat when I'm hungry (without having to " wait for lunch or dinner ") has also made that anxiety to relax and learn to differentiate the" physical hunger "of the" emotional hunger ". I do not have the feeling at any time of "being on a diet", but of having some routines and sticking to them as part of my day today.

It is important to note two things that have also been helpful to me whenever I have practiced intermittent fasting: on the one hand, the fact of being flexible, especially during weekends, when sometimes I do not comply with the same schedules as the days of diary. As I said above, it is important that the diet or, in this case, the nutritional strategy, adapts to us, and not us to it.

On the other hand, having a healthy diet most of the time with specific whims. Intermittent fasting is of little use, especially if we seek to improve our health through it if we base our diet on ultra-processed and other unhealthy products. Maintaining a healthy diet is essential if we want to achieve the benefits that this type of diet promises us.

CPSIA information can be obtained
at www.ICGtesting.com
Printed in the USA
BVHW011706180621
609641BV00015B/1167